76599

THE SENSE OF FORM IN ART

A Comparative Psychological Study

BY

H. WÖLFFLIN

TRANSLATED FROM THE GERMAN BY

ALICE MUEHSAM, Ph. D.

AND

NORMA A. SHATAN

CHELSEA PUBLISHING COMPANY
NEW YORK

PREFACE

T HESE THOUGHTS about "Italy and the German Concept of Form"[1] have been repeatedly taken up and laid aside again; finally prepared for publication, although in much abridged and often sketchy form.

The subject is more easily treated in the lecture hall than at the writing desk. The former offers the possibility of continuously supporting the spoken word with pictorial demonstration. Not only can more examples be shown, but variants and exceptions can be brought forward without danger of distracting the hearer, since the keynote may be immediately struck anew. Finally, the lecturer has in greater measure the freedom to make use of exaggerations for purposes of clarification (and entertainment), inasmuch as it is in his power to retract them at any moment. The written exposition, particularly if it is to be concise, does not allow of the same possibilities; it is therefore less stimulating and is more uncertain of success. The technique for such books still remains to be discovered. Nevertheless, even if the execution leaves something to be desired, the fundamental concepts in this book may be of some use in clarifying one of the most important problems of art history.

As regards the illustrations, every selection will appear fortuitous. I have imagined my readers to be such that it should be possible to speak of Raphael without supplying illustrations of the "School of Athens" or the Sistine Madonna; as for Dürer, the "Four Apostles" and "St. Jerome in his Cell" may be assumed to be familiar to everyone, just like his drawing of his mother and the "Great Piece of Turf." It would be desirable, of course, to be able to base such investigations to a still greater extent on single formal details, with

---

[1] The original German title, *Italien und das deutsche Formgefühl.* [*Tr.*]

comparisons of designs of hands, of clouds, of branches, down to
the design of the grain of wood—an art history of the smallest parts.
But this would result in a veritable atlas of form.

I have generally avoided the obvious procedure of demonstrat-
ing the national differences through the juxtaposition of contrasting
pictures. This method may well render good service in a lecture,
where it is possible to correct the one-sidedness of the single comparison by means of various other comparisons; but a well-grounded
misgiving kept me from making too extensive a use of this means
of elucidation in the rigid context of a book. After all, to wring a
specific effect of contrast from every picture does violence not only
to the reader but also to the work of art.

In the choice of illustrations (but not in the text), emphasis
is on the German side. One reason for this lies in the fact that the
works themselves are less known than the Italian; but the primary
reason is that the criteria for the interpretation of German art seem
to me to be less developed than for that of Italian art.

The entire subject of Italy is discussed solely in terms of its
significance for the Germans. This significance is, as is well-known,
so great that the history of German art cannot be fully dealt with
without referring to Italy. The relations of North to South, however,
are treated not historically, in terms of individual artistic personalities, but systematically, in terms of general form-psychological hypotheses. This book is intended to aid in the attainment of concepts
that are indispensable for a precise historical account. The writer
would be satisfied, however, if he were able to assist a few of the art-
minded travelers who annually visit Italy in understanding the
special attitude that Italy requires. It is a mistake to believe that
one can sit right down to dinner with the Italians. At best, the result
would be indigestion. The more often one goes to Italy and the
better one learns to know it, the stranger it will appear. And this is
as it should be. It may then happen that just such experiences will
make the voyager all the more clearly and vividly aware of his own
art at home.

The very definite line drawn here between German and Italian
art may seem to challenge the thesis of a uniform development of
European art; this frequently expressed thesis is also defended in
my book, "Principles of Art History." However, the contradiction

is only an apparent one. Such a general development is altogether compatible with a differentiated development of national concepts of form. All the same, a study in cross-section like the present one results in a more precise observation of the facts, on the basis of which I would today formulate a number of sentences in the older book somewhat differently.

I shall not go into the previous history of the studies included in the present book, since, as a purely personal concern, it would hold little interest for the general public. However, I cannot omit mentioning that these were the problems that formed the contents of the lecture given three years ago, at the invitation of the city of Nuremberg, on the occasion of the quadricentennial anniversary of Dürer's death. Since that time, I have frequently been asked why I have not had the lecture printed. Apart from the fact that an extemporaneous speech is not suitable for print just as it stands, it seemed to me that the subject called for a different, more leisurely discussion when intended for a reading public. What I had in mind can be seen in this book, which fell as a last, perhaps somewhat dried up, fruit from the tree of the year of the Dürer commemorative celebration.

ZURICH, 1931   H. W.

CONTENTS

LIST OF ILLUSTRATIONS

1. PAINTING AND GRAPHIC ARTS

2. SCULPTURE

3. ARCHITECTURE

PHOTOGRAPHS

INTRODUCTION

IN THE YEAR 1928, commemorative celebrations arousing wide-spread and active interest were held in honor of Dürer. If there was *one* motif that ran through all the speeches and writings inspired by the quadricentennial of the master's death, it was the acknowledgment of Dürer as the *greatest* German artist. It is unnecessary to reiterate either the grounds on which this acknowledgment was based or the qualities responsible for the time-defying vitality of his art. However, one is bound to be astonished that the greatest German master sought out Italian teachings in the decisive years of his life and that an art as foreign to his nature as the Italian was able to put him, the leading German artist, so strongly under its spell. By virtue of this, an antithesis dangerous to the native tradition inevitably arose. It was this that lay like a shadow on those commemorative celebrations. Even though the bold conqueror of distant foreign lands was being applauded, this Romanism could not but appear a disturbance of the natural development. The well-meaning admonition not to take these things too seriously is of no help. Dürer himself contradicts it—he *did* take Italy seriously.

Furthermore, it is not a question of a single case. A very large part of sixteenth-century German art manifests, in this sense, a Romanist attitude. Next to Dürer, Vischer's "classicistic" foundry was at work; and next to Nuremberg, it was above all in Augsburg that the Italian taste took root, from Burgkmair and Adolf Daucher down to the young Holbein. Holbein, who already belonged to another generation, finally welded Italian and German concepts of form into a union that had European validity. In point of fact, this Romanism produced a kind of split in German art. It is with good reason that Grünewald is felt to be almost generically different from Dürer—more popular, more closely connected with the native tradition of form. The same holds true for Altdorfer and Wolf Huber and—among the sculptors—for Backofen and Leinberger.

As a result, this relationship has been very bluntly expressed in modern art-historical terminology. The name German Renaissance is not, indeed, denied to the artistic circle with Italian affinities; but the other contemporary artists, such as Grünewald, are placed in decisive stylistic contrast to them by the designation "late Gothic artists" or representatives of a "late Gothic Baroque." A more radical proposal was to reject altogether the idea of a Renaissance for German art and to have late Gothic run directly into the Baroque.

In any case, the flowering of German art in the sixteenth century is said to be a phenomenon that cannot be compared with the Italian Renaissance. In Italy, one sees a uniform development on a modern basis from the Quattrocento to the classic art of the Cinquecento. In Germany, one finds in the sixteenth century a production that, retaining a connection with medieval Gothic, offers an equally brilliant spectacle; but, at the same time, the theory continues, sixteenth-century German art is permeated by a newly arisen trend, a trend essentially conditioned by outside influence, namely the Italianizing Renaissance. It was only logical that, accordingly, things were occasionally completely torn apart in the historical presentation and one piece found its niche in the Middle Ages, the other in the modern epoch. This is not to mention architecture, where it is customary to speak of a German Renaissance only from 1550 onward, i.e., after the close of the great age in painting and sculpture.

We cannot agree with this interpretation. To us, the great German art from the beginning of the sixteenth century denotes something unified and, in a similar sense, something classic like the Italian Cinquecento. In both countries, it was a period of the utmost creativity. Great talents existed in profusion, and eternal works of art came into being one after the other. Grünewald's Isenheim Altarpiece is contemporary with Michelangelo's Sistine Ceiling. And where else do we find a decade with the same abundance of overwhelming triumphs as the second decade of the century, even if only Dürer or Raphael are considered? The differences between the German masters, between Dürer and Grünewald, as great as they may be, pale into insignificance, or at least have no decisive importance, next to the new power of feeling common to all. Even though forms having their source in Gothic art were still used, there is a completely new wine in the old bottles. Thus, a secondary characteristic rather than a principal one is stressed by the term "late Gothic."

It is highly desirable that a generally satisfactory name for the great German period of artistic creation soon be found. In the present book, we do not altogether discard the old term "Renaissance"; but we use it reluctantly and only in the desire to create an awareness of the parallelism with contemporary Italian art, for which the term has come to be used. Dürer said *"Wiedererwachsung."* [1] Not very much can be done with that either. However, it seems intolerable to us to us the term "late Gothic Baroque" to designate the most vigorous and most robust art that German pictorial energy has produced. It is enough to make one lose one's appetite from the very start.

All the great German masters built on the "Gothic" fifteenth century in the same way that the Italian classic artists built on the Quattrocento primitives. The same problems occupied both countries. If the results are not the same, it simply means that each country dealt with the problems on a different basis—on the basis of a different concept of form, or on the basis of a different kind of imagination, which means the same thing.

One should not wait until the German style resembles the Italian to apply the name "Renaissance" to the North. The German and the Italian Renaissance *cannot* be the same. When a similarity did come about, that is, when Italian art took hold with greater exclusiveness, the "Renaissance" was in reality already over for the Germans.

Stylistic criteria taken from the actual formal content of architecture sometimes miss the essential point. Thus late Gothic and Renaissance architecture were by no means felt in Germany to be mutually exclusive opposites—the forms were used in combination with each other. This in itself proves that art-historical divisions and connections cannot be based on such factors. The presence of a Renaissance column offers no ground for postulating a special group in the history of German art, and the continued use of "Gothic" piers says nothing about a real spiritual connection with medieval style. The late Gothic body of forms is Gothic more in name than in fact. "Late" Gothic ornament should be understood as only in part the *late* product of a stylistic development; as for the other part,

---

[1] Literally "regrowth." [*Tr.*]

it comprised completely fresh imaginative forces that took over the traditional system of forms and used it as they pleased.

But even apart from architectural criteria—what is actually conveyed by calling Schongauer or Riemenschneider late Gothic artists? The connection with a development that stems from Gothic art can of course be demonstrated; but is not the newness of feeling more important than the connection with the past stressed by the name? Is it not precisely this new feeling that constituted the atmosphere in which lived not only Grünewald, but also Dürer—in fact, all the great German masters? This was not the stale air of a late art, but a new experience of form breaking forth out of the depths. When, down to the present day, the German spirit enjoys the play of interlacings, wild tree branches, roots, and broken drapery folds— who would want to call it a late Gothic fancy? These are age-old needs of the German imagination, which demand expression again and again.

In our opinion, the situation is more confused than clarified by the concept of late Gothic; and we should gladly see it used with more restraint. One obstacle to the comparative study of southern and northern art would thus be removed.

However, the following is of course still true: The picture of the German zenith does not possess the internal homogeneity presented by Italian art. In the latter, architecture, sculpture, and painting, uniformly developed, are in harmony with each other; and the various arts were often united in the selfsame person. When approaching German art, we must always be prepared for a co-existence of strong contrasts. Characteristic is the way sixteenth-century plastic art runs the whole gamut from the clarified tranquility and visibility of Vischer's sculpture to the almost inextricable vortex of forms of the Breisach altar. Plastic form meets with painterly form, and tectonic with atectonic, in a way that only the German will not reject as inherently contradictory. The interval spanned is so wide that, beside it, even Correggio suddenly seems very close to the classic Florentine and Roman masters, with whom he ordinarily appears at variance in every respect.

The contrasts, however, are not only distributed among different artists, but can also be found within the individual personality. Dürer gains his uniqueness—and German art its great depth—precisely by the fact that he unites in himself such contradictory elements: both characteristically northern traits and the feeling for values that had undergone a specific development in southern art.

With the foregoing, we again touch upon the problem of Italian art—the danger of Italian art.

To the Germanic people, Italy denotes something foreign to its nature. How was it possible that this country could nevertheless become model and destiny for Germany? Does that not imply self-renunciation? That German artists of the sixteenth century were oriented toward Italian art is a fact that cannot be shaken; nor is there a lack of criticism condemning the entire proceedings as apostasy of the Germans from their own individuality. But there is food for thought in the fact that their longing for the South, just as if they saw it as the land of promise, exactly coincided with the period of their own greatest creativity. It was the apocalyptic side of Dürer that was open to the vision of Italy. This was no search for foreign patterns out of a feeling of one's own weakness; rather, in the midst of the impetus of heightened creative power there arose the eager desire to conceive the world in a different way—in more definite shapes, in stricter conformity to rules, in more clearly visible form. The Germans saw the Italians to be well advanced along this path; how could they not have subordinated themselves to the latter as teachers? To be sure, a variety of inappropriate and misunderstood features were also transmitted, as always happens with imitation; but that has little importance, since the longing for Italy arose, after all, out of needs that had developed independently in the German spirit. If the Germans had not approached Italy with kindred vision, they would have been unable to see it. The spirit of a new interest in man and in objective form had seized the North as well. Thus, the Germans must have agreed in some way with Italy, to which this spirit is peculiar almost as a national possession from Antiquity onward, and where it had found comprehensive and overwhelmingly clear expression just during the Renaissance. Dürer had never intended to sacrifice German art to Italian art; he took whatever he needed, without letting himself be driven from the native soil in which his imagination was rooted.

From these considerations arises the problem under investigation: What is the Italian concept of form and to what extent can it be adopted by the North? We deal with the problem at only one point in history, which of course involves a certain narrowness of view; but since the period in question was the time of the strongest creative power on both sides, this analysis may have wider validity.

The concept of "Italy" is not a constant quantity, and the concept of "Germany" is even less so. Nevertheless, there is something that can be designated as a permanent national concept of form. We have become far too accustomed to divide the history of art into successive styles each of which is complete in itself. As a result, the incorrect idea that something completely new begins with each style has been able to creep in. However, only brief reflection is needed to realize that the various styles of a country do contain a common element that stems from the soil, from the race. Thus the Italian Baroque, for example, not only differs from the Italian Renaissance but also resembles it, since behind both styles stands the Italian man as a racial type; and racial types change only slowly. Such considerations are even more important for the North, because, with a less uniform stylistic history, the pervasive similarity of a national concept of form is all too easily lost sight of. Just the most distinctive buildings—say, of the German Baroque—derive their distinctiveness not merely from qualities that they have in common with the Baroque as a general style, but from much more basic motifs. And these motifs may reveal a concept of form that characterizes centuries of German art and that, under certain circumstances, may cause Baroque church architecture in Germany to appear related to German Romanesque.

On the other hand, an architectural group like the cathedral of Pisa and its campanile offers a contrast to contemporary German architecture on the order of the Abbey of Maria Laach, a contrast that asserts itself in a similar way as a national formal contrast throughout the entire history of art.

When we attempt to work out the artistic physiognomies of Germany and Italy in this way, we must not forget that nowhere do the peoples of Europe stand in opposition to each other as absolutely self-contained characters; rather, the soil everywhere is receptive to "the other" to a certain degree and, indeed, brings forth this other from within itself. Were this not so, people would be unable to understand each other at all. The relationship of Germany to Italy

was, to be sure, not reciprocal; it is impossible to imagine any of the
classic Italian masters setting out to drink of the northern artistic
spirit at its source. However, even classic Italy had an "anti-classic"
art; and Mannerism and the inherently painterly Baroque present
many possibilities of connection with the North. In such cases, the
question arises: What constitutes the "typical"? And this is certainly
even more apt to be sought in those instances where a nation is
unique and its creations untransferable. Italian Baroque churches
were able to gain admission into German cities without appearing
too strikingly foreign; the Farnesina or the courtyard of the Cancelleria would have remained incomprehensible. (That the histori-
cally-inclined artistic training of the nineteenth century finally
opened the doors to the whole world is another matter.)

For that very reason, we give less consideration in our demon-
strational material to those monuments that have been relatively
accessible to the German comprehension than to the totally different
type that has not been imitated and, indeed, has been scarcely seen—
less to the painterly buildings of Venice than to the severe Central
Italian architecture, less to Correggio than the painters of the classic
manner. We have essentially limited our German examples to those
from South Germany; this has its natural basis in the fact that the
decisive talents were almost all South German.

With regard to time, the years 1490 and 1530 may serve as rough
limits (apart from a few exceptions). They approximately embrace
Dürer's life-work and include the formation of Holbein's monumental style as well. In the realm of Italian painting, Leonardo's
"Last Supper" would represent the beginning of this period, and a
work like Titian's "Murder of St. Peter Martyr" the end.

However, as we have said above, the discussion will not revolve
about individual works of art, but about the basic concept of form;
not about art as such, but only about the premises of art.

I. FORM AND CONTOUR

To the traveler arriving in Italy from the North, the world appears all at once more tangible, simpler, and more definite. With what clarity the prism of the first campanile stands next to the church! How distinctly expressed are the proportions of the form of the church itself! What a simple cube is the villa on the hill of cypresses, as definite in its contours as are the nearby cypresses in form and direction! Everything, down to the single column, is firmly self-contained; and the forms seem set apart from one another in more explicit contrast than in the North.

We designate these characteristics the Italian plastic clarity; and surely the concepts of clarity and plasticity belong together, since the idea of plastic indistinctness makes no sense while the notion of painterly indistinctness is certainly a familiar one. However, two other points must be considered. First, we must not seek plastic clarity only where there is a question of solid form, of three-dimensionality. The quality we perceive as Italian in the organization of a façade or the wall of a room is the decisiveness with which the individual panels, pilaster intervals, or whatever planes there may be, assert themselves through their proportions, as do cubic forms. Thus the concept of plastic clarity is extended to include definitely limited form in general. At the same time, we feel that it is not so much a question of visual clarity as of a decisiveness of existence. We perceive an intense life in self-enclosed form. In the definite proportions of planes and solids, a self-contained life is revealed in its entirety. That is a great surprise for the northerner: that something alive can be embodied in stable proportions; that there is an art where content is completely contained within fixed form; that there are people who can fully express themselves in the visible.

However, there is more to be said. Once forms have attained completeness, they exist as wholly independent and self-sufficient entities. Therein lies an even greater surprise for the northerners. They come from a world of essentially different concepts, a world of the bound, the interdependent, the intertwined, where the individual form always remains more or less part of a greater whole. The individual part seems to come to life only in conjunction with many parts. The house is narrowly confined within its row on the street, and we can barely single out the church from its surroundings. In sculpture, the integration of the figure with architecture and the flickering rows of forms of a retable are much more characteristic than the free-standing figure. In painting, over-all movement, and not the individual form, stands out as the essential.

In Italy, the isolated figure, the isolated building, even the single column of a structure, are free to a degree unfamiliar to the Germans; and this freedom appears wonderful to them, as if it were a liberation, a deliverance. They then believe that they need only strip off their fetters in order to share in this freedom; but this is a delusion. The "plastic" ideal will satisfy their longing only momentarily; and then the German attitude to life will demand re-immersion in the element of the undefined and the not-wholly-independent, which remains involved in an infinity of relationships.

Limited form, fixed proportions, and distinct shape can never mean to the Germans what they mean to the South. The essence of German art is the impression of movement; and all movement refers to something outside itself. A general symbol of this conception of form could be the blazing fire. Just as single tongues of flame cannot be isolated, but merge with one another, so in this art, figure is tied to figure, form to form; and the imagination readily gives priority over the single motif to the over-all image of formal movement that is no longer linked to any objective meaning.

The proportion of each quality in the amalgam must always be considered. Of course, feeling for objective form is not completely lacking in this northern "painterly" viewpoint. And from time to time, this feeling predominated. These were the moments of heightened "plasticity" of perception, when suddenly the decisive quality was sought in the fixed and stable form of things and when the individual object was lifted out of the flow of movement to a more secure existence. The beginning of the sixteenth century was such a moment in the North. With Dürer, we see how proportion suddenly becomes of central importance. He even wrote a book: "Art of Measurement." All plastic epochs have been measuring epochs.

At such times, the North feels magically attracted to Italy and senses an affinity there. But German art did not become, and could not have become, Italianate. The alliance came about only with important reservations stemming from the traditional native concept of form. Dürer, with his plastic Romanism, represents, after all, only an extreme case; the national development proceeded along a different path. Nevertheless, Dürer is properly considered a central figure in German art rather than a peripheral one, since many anti-Italianate tendencies co-existed in him with those sympathetic to Italian aims. While Dürer surely patterned the horse in the "Knight with Death and the Devil" after Italian models, he created at the same time, in his "St. Jerome in His Cell," the interior space that provided a definitive answer to a specifically northern concern.

Such parallelism is typical for German art at its zenith. The case of Dürer, in which interests in plastic and painterly values are so widely contrasted, never recurred; but the polarity existed everywhere. In contrast to the fifteenth century, the feeling for the painterly approach was intensified in the same degree as the tendency toward measurable form deepened. Grünewald does not stand in complete contrast to Dürer. His painterly genius did not prevent his participation in the new plastic attitude of his time, but he had to make even greater reservations concerning Italian form than Dürer.

Plastic style implies a specific view of the world. Not only is the mode of seeing distinctive, but the content of the reality that is seen is itself different. If we can call Italy the land of plasticity, in a special sense of the term, we must surely admit that a particular natural world favored the development of this plastic conception. Nevertheless, it was not its sole source. We can look neither to the southern sun, nor to the soil and vegetation of the South for the explanation of the fact that, in Italy, the human figure dominates the image of the world. Everything is subordinated to it: "Man is the measure of all things" (a statement already used by Alberti in the form of a quotation from Antiquity). Since we can nowhere dismiss the psychological notion of sensibility [Einfühlung], we may say that the Italian sensibility differs from that in the North in that it is more precise, more form-directed. The North, however, has the capacity to enter into the spirit of that which lies both behind and beyond objective form, and to be transported from the well-defined to the undefined.

The basis of Italian pictorial art, as well as of architecture, is a highly developed appreciation of the body in terms of its proportions and possibilities of equilibrium. It is futile to try to work for the effects of Italian proportions as long as one does not have Italian bodily constitution. Only on this foundation could Bramante's architecture have been created, and a painting full of statuesque figures like the "School of Athens" could and can be understood only in these terms. To contrast this with something typically German: Germans will sooner recognize themselves in Dürer's engraving of St. Jerome, where, though the figure sits clearly in well-defined space, the emphasis is on an entirely different aspect, namely the over-all movement of the forms. This movement is carried not only by the material objects, but also, and quite essentially, by the flickering of the light. We experience this general movement of forms everywhere in the North—in the drawing of hands and feet as well as in that of a bush or a tree; in the drawing of waves in a body of water as in that of great atmospheric events in the sky. When Dürer, at the height of his plastic mastery, drew a foot (studies for the Heller Altarpiece), he stressed the animated cluster of forms and not the single configuration of each toe. Despite all his clarity in the representation of a leafy plant, a German artist can always be recognized by his perception of a secret life that goes from leaf to leaf and entwines one leaf with the next. Even the northern primitives saw more than a succession of single waves in a body of water: they were immediately inspired by the total complex of motion. And when clouds streak the skies, we can still perceive their connection with the earth, from which they have severed themselves as vapor. Even later on, Italian landscape painting always remained more or less bound to its "subjects," to the tree, the hill, the individual building. The Germans early manifested the tendency to gather all single objects together into one great current. Dürer produced landscapes from which all detail has been eliminated, landscapes that really contain nothing and seem to anticipate seventeenth-century Dutch spatial perception. ("View of the Environs of Kalkreuth.")

We can imagine how little Italian architecture, the art of bounded form, could accommodate an imagination thus disposed.

1.   Italian Architecture

When the aging Bernini traveled to Paris to build a palace for the King of France in the true—i.e., Italian—style, he began the conversation with an explanation of the fundamental importance of proportion. We may assume that he had previously reflected on the topic. With that explanation, Bernini hit upon the decisive point of contrast between Italian and northern architecture. That he represented the style we call Baroque is irrelevant: all preceding Italian concepts, in theory and in practice, proved him right.

In the North, the determining factor is what happens to and with form, rather than the fixed proportions of planes and solids; to northerners, movement is the essential quality. In Italy, however, a structure is primarily valued for what it *is*. Therefore the concept of proportion plays only a secondary role in the North; in Italian architecture (and not only in architecture) it is the key idea.

The first demand Italian architecture makes is that we focus on the effects of proportions and perceive the functioning of relationships in details and in the whole. Even today, the traveler can be advised to begin with such exercises, particularly when he finds Italian architecture bare and, so to speak, naked. In this nakedness, i.e., in severe form, the beauty is lodged. All else is secondary, and decoration can serve only to hide defects. Alberti had already stated this fundamental principle,[1] which remained decisive for the Renaissance and has, to a greater or lesser degree, been basic for all Italian art.

1.   Italy never ceased to value well-defined *surface proportions,* but during the Renaissance this type of beauty was consciously cultivated. The panel has new significance everywhere: in exteriors

---

[1] L.B. Alberti, *de re aedificatoria,* lib. VI. (beginning) . "ex his patere arbitror pulchritudinem quasi suum atque innatum toto esse perfusum corpore quod pulchrum sit." And earlier: "erit quidem ornamentum quasi subsidiaria quaedem lux pulchritudinis atque veluti complementum."

and interiors, in façades, walls, and ceilings, in tombs and choir-stalls. It has something to communicate. Its message, however, consists of nothing other than the most intensely felt life of definite surface extension, in harmony, of course, with the equally intensely felt total organism.

To illustrate, we point to the modest example (Fig. 1) of a tomb in the style of Desiderio da Settignano (Florence, S. Annunziata). What is there about it that looks so typically Italian? Evidently, the strongly stressed proportions of the planes, which need no decoration, since they are so meaningful in themselves. We see the three dark upright compartments into which the wall is divided, with the segmental niche over them; the harmony of these parts produces the full beauty, and yet each single element has its distinct value and self-sufficient existence. Certainly, special proportions were used that give the effect its particular inflection (the Renaissance had its own conception of beautiful proportions, which will be discussed later); however, there still exists the fundamental condition of a sensibility attentive to the self-enclosed plane.

Let us look at another example: the marble screens in the Sistine Chapel in Rome (Fig. 2). We are again immediately aware of proportion. The beauty of the Renaissance is fully realized in its simple elements: a lower wall-like panel and an upper grating between pilasters, in a pattern that repeats itself across the entire width of the chapel. The addition of decoration, as in the lower panels, basically does no more than underline the given proportions and make the beholder aware of them in a new way. The decoration not only leaves the precise effect of the proportions unimpaired but enhances it.

A motif of especial importance in the great secular architecture is the surface-articulating pilaster as used by Alberti in the Palazzo Rucellai (Florence). Its function can be interpreted as the organic animation of the wall; but its particular significance lies in its endowing the wall with proportional values. High Renaissance artists (Bramante, Raphael) used the motif in this way with the utmost vigor and believed, justly, that they had approximated the art of Antiquity. They sought their models in buildings like the Colosseum, where panels of incomparable distinction of proportion were created in the uppermost story through the distribution of pilasters. These

1. Florence

Tomb in
S. Annunziata

panels function, in a special sense, as measurable form; of course, everything architectonic must be measurable in some way, but here the measurements seem to lie exposed. A definite sense of existence was fully and purely realized in form.

We can find a German counterpart in the Ott-Heinrichs-Bau in Heidelberg. Here, despite the articulating presence of a supporting order in conformity with Italian models, a comparable effect is lacking, since the intervals between columns and pilasters have only little value in terms of proportion. The dominant charm of the façade lies in the rippling forms that flow over the entire surface. Although there is a new severity and the clear intention to achieve an Italian effect, the Italian system remains subordinated to a completely different set of goals. Beauty arising purely from proportion has little appeal to the German imagination; and thus it happens that façades in pronounced "Renaissance style" are essentially little removed from the "painterly" movement of a half-timbered wall. As a result, we are immediately aware of their kinship with these country cousins, now completely banished from the city.

2. Rome, Detail of Marble Screens in the Sistine Chapel

In Italy, Venetian architecture has always been considered want-ing in the feeling for proportion found in Central Italian architec-ture. This very lack explains why Germans have always been able to feel at home in Venice.

2. The difference in reaction to definiteness of proportion is also basically responsible for the distinction in the conception of *volume* in the North and in the South. Germans do not lack all feeling for volume; in the Frauenkirche in Munich or the Mauthalle in Nuremberg, the impression of volume, i.e., the perception of the great bodies as mass, was surely intended from the first. But it would occur to no one to want to measure. We are convinced that the primary significance of these structures does not lie in clearly com-prehensible proportions, but in their more-or-less undefined massiv-ity that calls for and admits of only an approximate comprehension.

Italian architecture, on the other hand, presents us with extremely clear solids, whose proportions are intended to be distinctly apprehended: only in this form could a definite attitude to life have found its lasting expression. Receptivity to proportion as such gradually developed in Germany as well, but even Renaissance architecture never became a *pure* architecture of proportion. The Town Hall of Rothenburg still retains an appearance of indeterminate form despite its more compact volume relationships; it could not exemplify Alberti's definition of beauty, which states that beauty resides in the thing itself and is not engendered by decoration.

Even today, the pure calculations of proportion in Italy will appear strange, at least to the unprepared. One wonders whether the Germans would have any confidence in a little church like Santa Maria della Luce in Perugia (Fig. 3) if it stood on their soil. It is nothing but a bare cubic form whose inner life is suggested by a few pilasters. Popular German taste would consider such architecture sober, bare, and impersonal. Why is this not so in Italy? Evidently, the harmony of proportions has a deeper emotional content there. However, special organs are required to perceive this harmony and to feel that such a church is not sober, bare, and impersonal. The simplicity of all classic[1] Renaissance architecture is founded on the idea that elementary cubic proportions are highly important and meaningful. The concave niche with or without a capping quarter sphere, used on a large scale by Bramante (Milan, Choir of Santa Maria delle Grazie; Rome, Belvedere Court) is a motif to which the northerner will at first respond with the feeling of a certain emptiness. Without being unreceptive to the effect of plasticity, he will experience the form as really alive only if something happens in or on the niche. An estimate of the difficulties that had to be surmounted in order for the Germans to arrive at an agreement with Italian art is afforded by Dürer's drawings like the one in color of the Virgin in an Italian hall (Basel), and even by Holbein's architectural settings. The physical sympathy, basic to all Italian art, which directly grasps the plastic content of a form and finds sufficient richness in the dis-

---

[1] "Klassisch." The words "classic" or "classical" usually refer in this book to the art of the High Renaissance. Any other meanings will be apparent from the context. [*Tr.*]

3. Perugia, Church of S.M. della Luce

tinctness with which the form reveals its meaning, is a rather un-common, though not unfamiliar, phenomenon for the North. We shall return to this later.

Here, too, the Renaissance found confirmation for its attitude in the remains of Antiquity. The juxtaposition of basic geometric forms—on a large scale in Hadrian's Mausoleum and on a small scale in the Tomb of Caecilia Metella—forms part of the fundamental impression of contrast received by the northern visitor. A cylindrical superstructure on a square base—and nothing else. A special plastic positiveness seems to give vigor to the forms.

3. Perhaps the most striking contrast between the two nations manifests itself in the *organization of space*. We can scarcely imagine today the degree of bewilderment experienced by the generation of Dürer and Grünewald upon emerging from its native Gothic hall churches into an Italian Renaissance interior. Even today, despite

all their historical training, the Germans feel something similar; and they should not suppress their spontaneous impression that something is missing in these spaces. The distinction is only vaguely characterized by the contrast of plastic and painterly concepts; the essential point is that the Germans do not conceive of space as fixed within definite limits and do not enjoy the beauty of fast and stable proportions. Instead, they desire to feel an intangible meshing in space. They seek less the proportions of self-contained space than the movement that pervades it and somehow always refers beyond it. For this, no Gothic nave is necessary; the same conditions hold true for ordinary low-ceilinged Gothic rooms: something spins down from the ceiling and stirs in the nooks and corners, which the Germans perceive as the true life of the space and do not gladly renounce in larger expanses. Furnishings do not matter (although they may greatly intensify the attractiveness of the movement); this distinctive quality, which is sensed like a confidential whispering, already resides in the purely architectonic forms of a church interior. By contrast, the beauty of proportion in a basilica by Brunelleschi demands an entirely new attitude. It is not impossible for the Germans to acquire this attitude; indeed, they may be strongly moved when, out of their sense of its differentness, they grasp the concept of circumscribed spatial extension in an Italian colonnaded hall or domed structure. These are moments of heightened physical sensibility; and during these moments there occurs, for the Germans too, that wondrous exaltation of the individual that alone renders this architecture comprehensible in its true sense.

With regard to the foregoing, it must not be forgotten that such definitions are condensations that should not be interpreted literally. The concept of limitedness is alien to no enclosed space and, conversely, the experience of movement is intended in all spatial forms. But our impression differs according to whether we grasp a spatial form purely and precisely, or perceive spatial extension only in that vaguer manner described above in relation to the exteriors of German buildings.

We point to the vestibule of the Cathedral of Pistoia (Fig. 4) as an illustrative example. Although photographs can never render space, which one must walk through and not merely see as a "view," the photograph of this simple hall-like expanse, with its solemn

4. Pistoia

Chiesa della
Madonna
dell'Umiltà.
Vestibule

barrel vault, may at least stimulate the recollection of the peculiar
effect of the precisely revealed, self-enclosed spatial proportions.

The Italian concept of space retained this character right up to
Bramante's St. Peter's and Vignola's Gesù. The Church of St. Michael
in Munich was patterned after the Gesù. Characteristically, it departs
from its Roman model in just the decisive feature under consideration—in the clearly perceptible proportions. We believe, it is true,
that we can survey the whole interior—the unified, barrel-vaulted,
longitudinal nave with its accompanying chapels; but every comparison reveals the contrast. The goal here was not fixed proportions,
but rather—how shall we put it?—a compelling whole. Thus the
individual parts, both inside and out, do not function as final self-
contained forms, but exist in a flow of pervasive movement.

4. This trait is most clearly expressed in the way the barrel
vault rests on the wall. We should expect the vault to be clearly
separated from the wall and to be placed on the wall as a distinct
piece, as if it were a lid. But the northern imagination avoids inde-

5. Padua, Palazzo del Consiglio

pendence of the parts: the vertical structure of the wall extends slightly into the vault, frustrating any attempt to perceive ceiling and wall as self-contained forms.

In Italy, the reverse is done. The view of the vestibule of the church in Pistoia demonstrates well the consequences of the principle of "definite form" for these parts. Not only is the vault self-contained in relation to the wall but, in addition, we are confronted with clearly expressed, well-defined entities, from the wall panels up to the coffers of the vault.

Even the columns and pilasters of Italian architecture are of pronounced plasticity—this last word always signifying distinct independent existence. If the pilasters and columns are chiefly responsible for the impression of lightness and articulation in southern buildings, other factors, to be discussed later, must also be considered, in particular their function within the whole. However, Alberti explicitly remarked that the isolated column retains its beauty just because it is a self-contained form. Of course, the degree of "plastic" treatment

6. Freiburg im Breisgau, The Exchange

is also important. All columns are not the same. Disregarding the North, where the column was always closely associated with the wall —even in Italy, which had never completely lost its Antique tradition, the form of the column underwent great change. The beauty it acquired during the Renaissance is rooted entirely in its plastic character, in the increased definiteness of its distinct existence. Those northern piers that somehow lose themselves as undefined form in the vault were absolutely unacceptable to Italian taste. In Germany, they were concurrent with Dürer's whole lifetime, a fact that even by itself indicates how basically different must also have been the painters' concept of form in the two regions.

Comparison of two approximately contemporary buildings, the Palazzo del Consiglio in Padua (Fig. 5) and the Exchange in Freiburg im Breisgau (Fig. 6), will clarify this distinction in every respect. The task was almost the same: a horizontal structure with

a closed upper story and an open portico below. The Italian portico
has columns (standing on pedestals) which support arches with
clearly molded archivolts and whose forms are easily isolable. In
the German portico, the piers blend into the wall with no definite
break and are of *one* piece with the wall; in addition, the indistinctly
inserted mouldings of the arches appear to be carved directly in the
wall. In a similar way, the oriels also are strangely dependent-
independent. They are rooted in the corner piers and surely project
as differentiated forms; yet they do not permit the spectator to
conceive of them as separate structures. Nothing analogous can be
found in Italy. With respect to the articulation of the wall, the Italian
example clearly reveals an intention not only to attain enclosed panels
(through the position of the pilasters) but also, and first and foremost, to dissect the structure into independent stories (by means of
the center cornice, which acts as juncture). In the Freiburg example,
the wall rises in uninterrupted movement: the balcony does not
function as a joint-like articulation. This tendency to conceive forms
in a unified flow still persisted in Germany even when the Italian
system of division by cornices had already become customary.

5. Proceeding to smaller and smaller things, we can further
demonstrate the principle of "definite form" all the way down to
ornament. A piece of Italian furniture (Fig. 7) is always characterized by its clearer design; and the same clarity of form is characteristic of an Italian printed page or inscription. This clarity will at first
appear to us as increased visibility and legibility; but it should not
be interpreted in purely optical terms. Instead, it must be traced
back to an ever-alert aspiration toward form, in the sense of a precise
perception of the world. The opposite can be seen in the flickering
northern "Gothic" script as used monumentally, and even as it was
handled by the classicist, Peter Vischer, who made the Kress epitaph
in the Church of St. Lawrence in Nuremberg. A completely different
conception of the eye and of the function of seeing is evidently basic
to this contrast, but also fundamental are different ideas about
beauty and happiness: here, the spirit of a dependent existence,
enmeshed in infinite connections, asserts itself along with the longing
and demand for a life of greater personal freedom.

Turning back from small things to great ones, we ought to

include the relation of building to site in our considerations. The image of the site of the Cathedral of Pisa, where the calm white marble structures of the Duomo, the leaning tower, and the baptistery stand next to one another on the green field, is unforgettable to everyone and will certainly be interpreted as specifically Italian. To be sure, this example is unequalled, even in Italy; but it can still be considered typical. We find something of this isolation in all great Italian architecture, whereas the North never lost sight of connecting elements and always experienced the relation between building and ground in a fundamentally different way.

2. Italian Pictorial Art

It has often been observed that the human figure was the true theme of Italian pictorial art. This is no doubt correct. Even Leonardo, who occasionally urged painters not to restrict themselves to the human figure as if the world did not contain a thousand other things, trees, rivers, cities, etc.—even Leonardo remained primarily a figure painter. However, it is not the numerical preponderance of the figure that determines the character of Italian art, but its distinctive interpretation. This feature is apparent immediately upon arrival in that country. The realm of isolated statuesque motifs begins. Diverse kinds of repose and movement are displayed with unfamiliar vigor. Not only is the system of the proportions of the parts more strongly stressed, but the body itself, by its balanced attitude and the organization of its limbs, becomes an artistic motif, without needing to have a more specific expression. This is related, of course, to the interest in the distinct and thoroughly sensed figure; but this definite and thorough sensing is not the result of systematic athletic training. It stems, in the final analysis, from a racially different bodily organization, in which the entire body becomes gesture. We find this trait in Germany only rarely, if at all.

1. The writings of Alberti contain the following sentence: "I have observed that if someone places his weight on one foot, then that leg always stands directly under the head." Alberti wrote this in 1435, in his treatise on painting. It is significant that this remark

7. Italian Furniture, ca. 1500 (Berlin, Kaiser-Friedrich-Museum)

was made by an Italian; one can imagine how strange it would look in a German treatise on art of this period (if any existed). To the plastically oriented Italian artists, however, these are the fundamental problems; even Leonardo, who admittedly saw the expression of emotion as the greatest glory of art, could say: "One of the most important aspects of the design of a figure is the correct placing of the head on the shoulders." Such words would be almost unthinkable on Grünewald's lips.

An early concern of Italian art theory was the exhaustive enumeration of the mechanical possibilities of bodily movement. Alberti had begun it—under the influence of the art theory of Antiquity—and Leonardo devoted many pages to the same subject. This concern may appear somewhat academic; but behind it lay a lively feeling for the wealth of plastic motifs, and it has to be seen in the context of southern life. (How fresh Alberti's words sound when he exhorts artists not to allow beauty to escape them, *quanto dolce le gambe a chi segga sieno pendenti!*) When Dürer took up the topic, it acquired a certain suggestion of formalism.

The significance of these broadly formulated southern varieties of movement is clarified a hundredfold in large-scale narrative frescoes. Benozzo Gozzoli was not one of the greatest artists; yet how vivid is the action throughout his paintings and how impressive the single motif! In the fresco of Noah's drunkenness in the Campo Santo in Pisa, he depicts the vintage: the man on the ladder who hands down the basket, the woman standing with upraised arms ready to receive it, and all the other motifs gathered together there in inexhaustible succession. In all these inventions, we sense the artist's joy in the plastic themes as such; and no one was disturbed if, once in a while, the interest in form received preference over the demands of the subject. But all the experimentation of the Quattro-cento artists is, after all, only a tame prologue when compared to what the sixteenth century and Michelangelo brought in wealth and magnificence to thematic invention. Let us disregard his narra-tive paintings: even the seated pairs of "slaves" in the Sistine ceiling are figures that strain to the utmost the imaginative power of the spectator wishing to master their plastic content. The impact is heightened by the fact that the motif is composed not of a single figure but of a *pair* of figures with complementary or contrasting movements. (An important defect of many illustrated books is that they neglect this duality and reproduce only the single figure torn from its context.) Even very simple seated or standing figures are rich in contrasting directions to a degree unfamiliar to the Germans. Indeed, a certain training is necessary to comprehend these formal combinations fully and, above all, to appreciate their true value. In motifs of stance like that developed by Leonardo for example, where one foot is raised and the hips turned, while an arm reaches across the body and the head turns in the opposite direction—in these poses, the Germans may easily see only external exaggeration that threatens to be transformed at any moment into artificiality or mannerism. The Italians, however, set the boundary between arti-ficiality and naturalness at a different point and, from the beginning, felt that, through greater formal richness, life was also enriched. It may be argued in individual instances whether the artist's vitality was adequate to the requirements of the formal scheme; but there is no doubt that contraposto was frequently understood in Italy as the expression of heightened ideality. Looking at the over life-size seated figure of an Evangelist (St. Mark) by Fra Bartolommeo in the Palazzo Pitti (Fig. 8), the northerner may consider its display of

8. Fra Bartolommeo, St. Mark the Evangelist (Florence, Pitti)

movement unmotivated, and therefore empty; and he will readily contrast it with a work like Dürer's St. Paul in the Munich Pina-kothek, where the motifs of corporeality and plasticity are almost non-existent. Such criticism, however, is nationally conditioned; and it is an extremely delicate problem for a German to judge at which point Italian form passes over into formulism.

2.   In Italian art, we are always aware of the solid body under its clothing. Alberti only put into words a generally recognized concern when he charged the artist to draw every figure first in the nude and only then to think about the garment. This injunction should

9. Donatello, David (Florence, Museo Nazionale)

not be interpreted as the pedantry of a theorist. We learn from many
examples that the method was generally applied, not only by Raphael, whose use of it we take for granted, but even by Baroccio,
in whose hands it seems strange and unnecessary. Even when this
technical aid was not employed, the Renaissance always made certain
that the essential points of bodily articulation were not hidden from
sight. Even a painter of the early period like Filippo Lippi—who had,
moreover, no great personal interest in anatomy—always treated the
kneeling angel of the Annunciation in such a way that the position
of the important joints can be determined with certainty. In this
attitude lies one of the most radical differences between southern

and northern art. Jan van Eyck may have greatly advanced the process of graphic execution; but his kneeling Gabriel in the Ghent Altarpiece leaves us completely in the lurch with regard to structure. Later, different requirements were set up in the North as well, and drapery folds were no longer all-important. But even where the form is more clearly indicated, body and garment still remain an inseparable whole. How little sense it would make to convert Dürer's great St. Paul into a nude! (See St. Catherine in Fig. 15, an exception to this.)

The Italians seem to have felt that ancient art required the awareness of the body beneath the garment. We learn this from a remark by Vasari in reference to Donatello's Annunciation relief in Santa Croce, as well as from other sources.

It was only logical that finally the anatomic structure beneath the skin should also be rendered visible. The first artist-anatomists appeared in Italy. But all anatomic thoroughness in rendering the figure was again only the result of a more intense interest in the body, and aimed less at an objective statement of the facts as such than at sharpening the impression of form; for this, Michelangelo should be cited as the principal example. By his treatment of the joints alone, he put an end to the entire fifteenth-century manner of drawing. He found fault with Dürer's treatise on proportions for neglecting the anatomical substructure.

3. Alberti had earlier expressed the opinion that the draftsman should always go back to the anatomical foundations of the figure; even then these words had a particular meaning, namely that only anatomy offers sure starting points for the evaluation of body proportions. Prerequisite for an interpretation based on proportion is the clear differentiation of all parts of the body. A head is described as plastic if the single forms are precisely defined and set off from one another with easily perceptible clarity. The same holds true for the torso and the limbs. We cannot further concern ourselves here with the extent to which Antiquity acted as a clarifying and elucidating force (Michelangelo's "David," with its punctuating accents, would be inconceivable without ancient models); the *essential* factor in this regard is that the plastically conceived body was understood as a problem of proportion from the very beginning. The concept

of measurability was of prime importance in the pictorial arts, as in architecture. The numbers (obtained from the average of many measurements) that Alberti set down in his treatise *de statua* as criteria for the perfect human body need not be considered absolutely binding; but it is an important fact that measuring took place at all and was considered primary rather than incidental. Even where actual numerical tables are absent, we may assume that the artist "had the compass in his eye," to use Michelangelo's expression. Although it was not used at all times and in a uniform way, it would be strange if this gauging of proportions, practiced at every turn in the field of architecture, should have been omitted in regard to the organic form.

Here again, the Italians were in accord with Antiquity. It is not accidental that Donatello's classicizing bronze of "David" (Fig. 9) is at the same time a figure decidedly based on proportion. From here, the line proceeds down to Bandinelli's "Adam and Eve" (1551) from the Duomo in Florence (Fig. 75); they are large figures that the northern traveler finds uninteresting, since they strike him as empty and inexpressive. Vasari, however, praised them expressly on account of their proportions. We need not stress that the accessible Venetian beauty, the reclining female nudes by Giorgione and Titian, must also be understood in the first place as a beauty of proportion and as a harmony of form; and the more definitely the individual components of this harmony assert themselves, the stronger its effect will be.

Italian art theory demanded at the start, and repeatedly afterward, that the artist know the measurements of each part of the body (and how they relate to one another.)[1]

This concern is unfamiliar to the Germans; for them, the value of form lies more in its function than in its fixed proportions. Although Dürer was passionately involved with the problem of proportion, the stimulus admittedly came to him from Italy. The novelty of the matter is reflected in the powerful impression he had on first seeing figure design as a question of proportion. However, this concern could never achieve primary importance for the North.

---

[1] Alberti, *della pittura* III.: "ne sarà parte alcuna della quale non sappi suo officio e sua misura."

How many German figures can be said to have the quality of measurability? There are a few, but they are exactly the ones we can most easily do without. The others will not submit to the compass.

4. As we have seen above, the human figure and the plastic motif must be credited with a particular significance in Italian art. To complete this statement, we must add that the human figure appears there in isolation and more or less maintains its independence within all combinations. Every plastic style is an isolating style. All is clearly separated: form is distinct from form, figure from figure. Furthermore, the figure is also kept separate from the landscape background or architectural space. As soon as the plastic sensibility sets in, we come to the end of the serried rows and groups that distract attention from the individual object. (These, incidentally, were not foreign to Italian Gothic.) Each form is then presented as a self-sufficient independent entity, in both architecture and the pictorial arts.

Here we find the principal cause of the sense of liberation experienced by the northerner in Italy. Even the most cursory comparison makes us aware of how few free-standing figures there are in Germany; of how everything (completely apart from the mode of execution) is somehow dependent and interlocked; in short, how all is bound up in a larger context from which it cannot be released—not even in thought.

The contrast is most clearly revealed in the juxtaposition of the Italian niche, in which the figure moves with complete independence, with the northern canopy and column figures, which never seem capable of living entirely in their own right. The North was in no haste whatsoever to strip off these "Gothic" bonds (did it ever wholly do it?); in the South, the ties were looser from the start. What was the status of the free-standing figure in Germany? Evidently, the North's plastic needs were completely satisfied by the rows of figures on the dark retables. Later, the close involvement was loosened and the single motif received stronger emphasis; but we can sense the difficulty that the Germans had in parting with the idea that the retable was not only a sheltering cover for the figures but was altogether necessary to them as *"Lebensraum."*

When a figure in free silhouette, in the Italian manner, occasionally turns up, some mysterious magic effect seems to have vanished.

In Italy, the devotional image is a figure composition in which the plastic motif is clearly evident in each figure; and a *conversazione profana* with many figures, like the "School of Athens," is nothing other than an extremely artful unity of persons and groups, which nevertheless remain isolable. The relation of figure to space is no different from that between figure and niche: they function together harmoniously, but each pictorial component remains an entity in itself. We can well imagine that such architecture was first designed as a stage upon which the figures were then placed. In the entirely different German conception, figure and space form an indivisible complex, just as there is no such thing for the Germans as a figure that is first drawn nude and then clothed.

We can clearly see the point at which the Italian discipline begins to be adopted. However, the plastically clear, stage-like spaces, seen and constructed for their own sake, betoken great danger for the naturalness of the German imagination. Here, everything depends on the experiencing of space and its contents as a unity, so that the elements appear inseparable even when each one is very clearly worked out. In such peculiarities of artistic imagination lie the reasons that a "St. Jerome in His Cell" was possible for the Germans but not for the Italians. What oneness of figure and atmosphere! The saint is like a spider in a web of lines and lights that is as indispensable to his existence as he is to the web.

3.   German Pictorial Art

1. Plasticity is the keynote of the sixteenth century in the North as well. The human figure becomes weightier, both literally and figuratively. Volume is more strongly felt, and the body is thoroughly sensed in terms of structure and equilibrium. The nude appears. Suddenly we encounter people who have become aware of their own bodies. Riemenschneider's "Adam" may still wear his nudity like an unfamiliar garment, but it seems that only now had people truly grown into their bodies.

We may consider it natural for representational art to take the

10.
Hans Beierlein

Tomb Plaque
of Bishop
H.v.Lichtenau.
After 1505
(Augsburg,
Cathedral)

single figure as its starting point, a view to which Dürer's example
seems to give strong support. Nevertheless, the facts teach us that
the North was of a different opinion. The primary element was not
the figure as such; instead, the northern conception was determined
by the figure complex, by the interconnection of the form and its
surroundings. It was a long time before the motif of the single body,
as conceived by the Italians, could achieve importance; and by that
time the German Renaissance was almost over.

In the Cathedral of Augsburg, there is a depiction of the "Agony
in the Garden" on a tomb plaque for Bishop H. v. Lichtenau. The
artist, Hans Beierlein, was not one of the leading men; but his work
is in no way behind the times. From this relief, we can well ascertain

the intermediate state of the German concept of form at the beginning of the sixteenth century. We see Christ kneeling against the
rocks. Below, St. Andrew, with his diagonal cross, presents the bishop.
On the left, above the bishop's escutcheon, we see St. Peter and St.
James; at Christ's back is St. John and, in the background, the pro-
cession of captors. The enclosing arch contains clouds and little
angels holding the cross; and finally, completing and framing the
rest, are figures of prophets in the spandrels. This is approximately
how an objective description of the plaque should run. In reality,
the eye at first sees something entirely different, namely an agitated
wave-like surface where, here and there, a thematic detail becomes
more or less distinctly visible. The foremost artistic concern was
not the clear and plastic rendering of the figure but rather the
"painterly" movement of the aggregate of crowded bodies, landscape,
and framing corner figures. The garments with their abundant sharp
folds are very important in this connection. Northern drapery is not
understood if its function as a *carrier of movement* goes unperceived.
The modern spectator may have good reason to complain about lack
of clarity. Presumably, eyes were differently trained at that time;
but, in addition, people basically wanted to see something different.

Nothing is more instructive than the contemporary drawing of
a sculptured work such as the one in Basel by Holbein the Elder
(Fig. 11) after the Mörlin memorial plaque (Augsburg Cathedral,
Cloister). This interpretation in which the forms are so entangled
may be regarded as completely typical, even though probably not
every artist would have carried it so far.

If the great masters of the sixteenth century then sought a more
positive statement of plasticity, it does not mean that the "painterly"
interpretation was to be eliminated: it was developed further but,
at the same time, was fused with its opposite. Therein lies the peculiarity of the German style. The greatest stylistic contrasts, like Peter
Vischer's classicism and the entanglements of the Breisach Altar,
thrive next to one another. Between them, however, stands the art
of a Backofen with its magnificently clear plasticity, which maintains
itself against the powerful breakers of a swirling surf of form.

The same holds true for the graphic arts. If we juxtapose the
style of Dürer's woodcut of the "Apocalypse" with the type of sculpture that treats a relief like a piece of tilled land—in Nuremburg,

11. Hans Holbein the Elder, Drawing after the Mörlin Memorial Plaque in the
Cloister of the Augsburg Cathedral (Basel, Kunstsammlung)

the comparison with Veit Stoss or the younger Adam Krafft is most
apropos—we then realize that representation in Dürer's work de-
velops more and more toward plasticity and distinctness. But it does
not lose its substratum of formal entanglement. We see this demonstrated in the fully mature woodcuts of his classical style, where
the painterly element still vibrates like a persistent undertone. But
even a single drawing like the portrait of his mother of 1514
is sufficient illustration. Although produced at the height of the
plastic domination of form, this drawing is not at all comparable to

12. Adam Krafft, Pergenstörffer Memorial Relief, ca. 1498
(Nuremberg, Frauenkirche)

Italian art, because of the interweaving of the forms and the snake-like winding of the lines, as in the ribs of a late Gothic vault.

And yet, within German art, Dürer represents the plastic and not the painterly pole.

2. We shall first examine the relation of picture to *frame* as one of the conditions for the peculiar dependent-independent effect of the figure in Germany.

Everyone knows Riemenschneider's magnificent figures of 1493, Adam and Eve from the Würzburg Marienkapelle and now in the

Luitpold Museum of the same city. They are among the most precious possessions of German art; but their original effect vanished when they were removed from their architectonic frame. Flanking the portal, they originally stood on pedestals under high canopies made by Riemenschneider himself. Such architectonic crownings are not merely decoration that may just as well be omitted. They are wholly essential to the figure: the figure is incomplete without its canopy. This elevated form hovering over the head of the figure kindles the flame of the upward-licking movement. Divested of this accent, the figure shrinks or, if this is saying too much, it acquires a shivering frailness in a degree that was surely not intended by the artist. (The pedestal, of course, was also included in the total effect; and certain forms, like the now somewhat prominent fig-leaves in the middle of the figures, served only to transmit the painterly movement from the rich forms of the base to the canopy.) (See Figs. 30 and 31.)

It is only by chance that we are so well-informed here about the original arrangement. How many figures, now standing incomprehensible in museums, should also be similarly completed! The feeling for the effect of the original ensemble has been almost completely lost. In illustrations, too, a one-sided interest has led to the practice of tearing the figure from its context, even where the original whole still exists. To be sure, a work like the Pergenstörffer memorial relief (Fig. 12) by Adam Krafft (Frauenkirche, Nuremberg) would not be illustrated today without its framework, as if only the figures mattered.[1] Depicting the Virgin standing and crowned by angels, the composition achieves a truly hymn-like intensification just through the *élan* of the enclosing canopy. However, the times when this was done are not too far past; and more recent illustrated books indicate that attention is really still focused on the figure alone.

It is certainly true that the trend of the time was toward greater independence of the figure. The apostles of Vischer's St. Sebald Shrine stand with greater freedom under their canopies; and the entire generation thought differently about the relation of sculpture to its framing architecture. But the traditional main theme of sculpture

---

[1] Bode, *Geschichte der deutschen Plastik,* 1886. Here we find a woodcut, made after Riemenschneider's "Last Supper" in Rothenburg, that omits the framing elements and the background.

—the shrine with figures at the altar—held its ground. The bonds loosened somewhat and the individual figure gained more independent significance; but it still remained more or less interwoven in the row of figures and entangled in the tectonic-vegetative casing of the Shrine stand with greater freedom under their canopies; and the en-aspect. Whether the saints seem to sit in ivy or rose arbors, or whether, standing in narrow grooves, they are borne on a powerful all-inclusive current that culminates in an upward-rushing "geyser," the final result always transcends the figures. Only when they are carried on a wave of architectonic-decorative forms do the figures become all they are meant to be. Not only does the shrine serve as an effective foil to the figures (in a painterly sense, as well, through the darkness in the depths of the shrine); it also raises them beyond themselves. They are endowed with life by something that is external to them.

Leinberger shared Riemenschneider's attitude in this regard; and the plastic figures of the Isenheim Altarpiece, although highly meaningful in themselves, cannot be removed from their setting without losing their essential qualities. We cannot say the same of an Italian Renaissance niche figure.

The concept of a figure that is able to exist only within a larger formal context was difficult to uproot in the North. The free-standing figure gained ground only gradually and against resistance; and yet in this change lay the basis for the development of plastic values. But it is curious that, as soon as artists, impressed by Italian models, felt obliged to proceed more radically, a certain quality of emptiness entered their work. The effect of Peter Vischer the Younger's tomb (Wittenberg, 1527) for Frederick the Elector of Saxony is so much colder in its statuesque completeness than the "Gothic" tomb his father had made for Archbishop Ernest in Magdeburg (1495). In the latter, the movement of the figure is continued in the accessories; and under the impact of an ideally heightened life, the spectator finds it impossible to judge how much of much of this impact derives from the figure alone. (A contrasting Italian example might be Pollaiuolo's almost contemporary reclining tomb figure of Sixtus V in St. Peter's.)

A similar problem existed in painting as well. The concept of the self-contained panel, which seems so natural to us, was only

13. Talheim Altarpiece (Stuttgart, Schlossmuseum), School of Ulm, ca. 1510

Unity of figures and frame. Similar movement in drapery folds and canopy. The raising of the central part is indispensable to the figure of the Virgin. For discussion of the inclusion of the side canopies in an over-all form, see Chapter III.

gradually accepted by German artists. The museums do not offer completely reliable information on this subject. Apart from the dismemberment of complexes of paintings intended to be judged as ensembles, such as the great altarpieces, there are single paintings that have been divested of their old carved tracery and provided with new frames. It makes a difference whether or not a panel had, from the first, its distinct value as a surface area, i.e., whether it was a complete entity in itself, or not. It can be proved in many cases, and surmised in others, that the panel was, in fact, not a complete entity. For example, the paintings of the Life of Mary in Munich by the so-called "Master of the Life of Mary" once had tracery, and would be extraordinarily improved if the corners were again filled in—the composition was designed with this in mind. This filling-in of the spandrels cannot be considered a bad habit of the primitives: we find them again in Dürer's "Adoration of the Trinity" and, on a very large scale, in Baldung's high altar (Fig. 14) in Freiburg im Breisgau. Whether the artist envisioned a rectangular panel or one with an arched top is not pertinent here; the point is whether or not the painting has need of ornament in the spandrels. It seems certain to us that the impression is a much more sober one when it is missing. We may be unfamiliar with a concept of painting in which picture and frame are thus coordinated; yet the fact remains that the great artists of the sixteenth century accepted it. However, this barred neither the concurrent production of self-sufficient panels nor the feeling of certain painters that the traditional tracery was beginning to be burdensome.

3. Razor-sharp boundaries and exact measurability characterize not only Leonardo's "Last Supper" but also earlier Quattrocento interiors; and northern interiors will always appear more or less unintelligible in comparison. However, the lack of emphasis on limits in the North is only a concomitant of the impression of all-embracing movement. The nature of this movement is such that the space enters into a peculiar union with all its contents, both animate and inanimate. Space and figure are not two separate entities but function together as a unity. This relationship continued even when the sixteenth century, with its more acute plastic needs, undertook to make space more precise in the geometric sense. We surely do not choose a

14. Hans Baldung, High Altar of the Cathedral in Freiburg im Breisgau. 1512-1516

The painting is complete only when in its frame. The frame, without being an actual extension of the picture, continues its movement. Furthermore, the composition takes into account the complementary contrast of the wings (standing apostles, closely pressed to one another).

15. Albrecht Dürer, Madonna with Saints. Drawing of 1511 (Albertina)

The peculiar relationship of figures to architecture is rendered even more acute by
the strong perspective diminution of the figure of the Madonna and by the obliqueness
of the space.

Adoration
in the Stable
(Munich, Alte
16.   Pinakothek).
Hans Baldung   1520

particularly favorable example when we support this assertion with
a drawing by Dürer depicting the Virgin with saints (1511) in an enclosed vaulted hall (Fig. 15), a drawing from his middle period and
showing Italian influence. But despite the obvious dependence on
Venetian religious painting, there is an entirely un-Italian quality in
the way the figures are made to conform with the space, like a mussel
in its shell, instead of being inserted into a prepared expanse.

This is true to an even greater degree of Grünewald's painting
of the Annunciation in the Isenheim Altarpiece. Without being able
to say that the chapel is somehow unreal or even unclear, we believe
ourselves to be confronted by a living, breathing being, whose pulse
beats in time with that of the figures. This, of course, denotes something entirely different from the harmonious relationship of a self-
sufficient Italian architectural space to statuesque self-contained
figures.

If we think of a picture like Dürer's "St. Jerome in His Cell," where light has become a truly active element, we then realize the suitability of the over-all movement that conditions the specific mood. Nothing is indistinct; nor are there the waves of light and dark we later find in Rembrandt. All the forms are clearly defined; but the way in which tangible and intangible elements, shadowed and illuminated figures, join in a unified movement produces an atmosphere for the saint that no longer has any analogies on Italian soil.

The Germans loved ruins because of this very quality of movement. This love manifests itself in remarkable fashion in the works of Baldung (Fig. 16) and Altdorfer where the Holy Family is sheltered within decaying walls. Here, objective form has little significance, and the non-objective and accidental hold sway. The forms then come into unexpected combinations and among them arises a mysterious whispering; it is truly a wonderland. The minor role accorded these motifs by Dürer is characteristic of the plastic nature of his art. His architectural settings all tend toward bounded form, even when they are meant to be "romantic"; and in the Paumgärtner Altarpiece, there is actual stiffness. To the Italians, however, the poetry of ruins is as good as unknown. They, too, have ruins; but to them it simply means that a column is broken off, or that a piece is missing from a wall. The Italian sense of objective and distinct form maintains itself in their impression.

From ruins to natural landscape is only one step; the contrast remains the same. The German feeling for landscape differs from the Italian in its more intense awareness of a total coherence. This awareness is not absent in Italy but is of a different kind: it is more the perception of the juxtaposition of things than of their interplay. In the northern landscape, clouds and earth, trees and bushes, the hill and its crest merge together in an all-pervasive sensation of life and motion. Paintings by Altdorfer and Huber bear ample witness to this quality. Even a detailed representation like Dürer's "Great Piece of Turf" can be understood only in terms of the mood of this kind of landscape. Although Dürer, according to his personal bent, presents the plants in distinct and orderly fashion, they nevertheless seem to whisper to one another. The interweaving of existences and the feeling for the life of an unbounded formal whole are the essential elements.

The northern talent for this kind of interpretation becomes

17. Hans Burgkmair, Drawing for a Painting (Berlin). 1505

manifest in the peculiar bond between the human figure and the landscape. Earlier in this chapter, we referred to a relief depicting the Agony in the Garden in which figures and setting merge into a unified surface movement not exactly conducive to clarity of appearance. We can amplify the point with a work in the advanced style of the sixteenth century: a preparatory drawing by Burgkmair (Fig. 17) of the same theme, in which the clarity of the figures is heightened. Everyone will recognize that the pictorial principle has remained basically the same. The Agony in the Garden is still conceived as a whole which is not dominated by the figures, but in which figures and landscape are inextricably interlaced.

The principle may become less rigorous, but it will not disappear as long as the national tradition lasts.

18.
Martin
Schongauer   St. Sebastian

4. Dürer's drawing of Adam and Eve of 1504 (Fig. 27) must
have appeared even stranger to his contemporaries than is usually
assumed. The Italian motifs of movement are not its most interesting feature; but a new world was opened up to the North by these
self-contained figures who, as independent and complete beings, are
regulated by their own inner laws. From their Gothic churches,
northerners knew only interlocked forms, where neither surface, pier,
nor figure had really independent significance. Thus, Dürer's drawing revealed to them an entirely different concept of art and an entirely different interpretation of the universe, in which free, self-reliant figures have their value in themselves and reveal themselves
through their own form.

We know that Italy served as the model for this innovation.
However, the important point is not the Italianism of this drawing
as an isolated outcome of study but the fact that a great wave of feeling for plasticity arose at that time in the North as well. Dürer could

not have been interested in Italian form had his own approach not been related. The scholarly quality still adhering to the engraving of 1504 gradually vanished. And when Cranach and Baldung took up the theme of the human body, they moved even further away from the Italian manner, and the connection with the fifteenth-century attitude becomes apparent. This attitude, however, was opposed to limited form.

A figure like Schongauer's "St. Sebastian" (Fig. 18) demonstrates well what we mean. The body is so closely entwined with the tree that it looks as if it were frayed. We are in no doubt as to what is body and what is tree; but it would be difficult to separate one from the other. The plastic value of the body plays only a minor role within the total complex of forms composed of body, branches, and fluttering loin cloth. The engraving lacks the concentrated awareness of the body that gives strength to every Italian St. Sebastian and prevents it from being perceived as forming a unit with accompanying forms. In German painting and sculpture, on the other hand, the body easily loses itself in its accessories.

This feeling for defined-undefined form must be still taken into account as a basic psychological fact in the sixteenth century. Baldung produced drawings of nudes with strongly agitated draperies that, despite their stress on corporeality, are in line with Schongauer's "St. Sebastian." These drawings do not contain bodies around which a cloth is fluttering; rather, part of the plastic form flows off into the garment. (What a powerful and indispensable aid the wind has been in German art!) If we compare Grünewald's Sebastian in the Isenheim Altarpiece with Schongauer's figure, we again find a fundamental kinship. True, Grünewald's figure is filled with a new feeling for the body, and its movement is rich in contrasts; but we would seek in vain for an Italian equivalent (Michelangelo's "Christ with the Cross" has been mentioned in this connection), since the conception of the figure certainly does not rest on a pure plastic basis. The figure does not live entirely on its own; instead, the trailing mantle is an integral part of the form.

This also explains why, in Grünewald's painting of the Resurrection, the body of Christ fails any test of its plasticity: the sensibility to and thorough awareness of the body as such is lacking; and the effect depends on the total impression of ascending movement, on the trailing draperies and everything connected with them. Condemning it as mere *"Brauch,"* [1] Dürer rejected this manner; but in it, the popular taste found its needs and desires well satisfied.

The presence of the idea of the plastically and clearly conceived body in Germany during the sixteenth century must be largely, if not exclusively, credited to Dürer. Yet how curious it is: wherever the figure is represented for its own sake in German art, the impression of movement always overshadows the impression of mere being. No accompanying "alien forms" deny the figure the effect of clarity; but the play of great curves and counter-curves in the design still engulfs a good part of the interest in bodily proportions, structure, and equilibrium.

The Germans, too, feel the desire to turn from indefiniteness and movement to pure form, but they cannot give up the fundamental basis of plastic indistinctness and intangibility. They consider this basis not as something to overcome but as the maternal soil from which pure form occasionally arises. A world in which everything existed in equally clear and plastic form would, in the long run, be unbearable for them.

Even to Dürer, the strictest of German figure painters, the human form could never be what it was to the Italians: the vessel in which the entire contents of the world were collected. To Dürer, it was only *one* form of life, even if the most significant.

For the North, the real person is the *clothed* and not the nude person. The Italians, too, knew how to endow the figure with vigor, fullness, grace, or nobility through drapery; but, from the outset, the body was felt to be the bearer of the garment. In German art, the garment may have an absolute value in itself. The splashing masses of folds of Schongauer's "Virgin Seated in a Garden" are the bearers of a main share of the mood; and it would occur to no one to want to establish the form of the figure beneath the drapery. Even in the sixteenth century, when more rigorous demands were made in regard to an objectively comprehensible relationship between body and garment, plastic clarity never became a universally binding rule, and

---

[1] As used by Dürer, *"Brauch"* refers to practical skill or practice, as opposed to theoretical knowledge and insight. See Erwin Panofsky, *The Life and Art of Albrecht Dürer* (Princeton, 1955) , pp. 164 and 242. [*Tr.*]

18 a
Master in
Augsburg

St. Anne
and the
Virgin,
ca. 1520
(Berlin)

vagueness always remained influential to a certain degree. The magnificent deluge of Leinberger's drapery (Fig. 19) does define the body; but one must not inquire about the shape of the mantle or the mechanics of its folds. Dürer, whose plastic sense was the most alert, did not hesitate to completely subordinate the figure to the garment, even in a monumental figure like that of St. Paul in the painting of "The Four Apostles"; here, only the cloak speaks. Nevertheless it is at least *possible* to project a body into this powerful covering. In other cases, it is not possible. Peter Vischer's figures of knights in Innsbruck, the best known free-standing figures of sixteenth-century German art, are called "armor come alive" by one of Vischer's biographers (Meller); the reason is that it is absolutely impossible to imagine an organic body conforming to the armor. If this was permitted in classic sculpture, what can we expect from mere drawing, which always laid claim to the right to greater unreality? Taken seriously from the plastic point of view, the bodies in Baldung's woodcut series of apostles would have to be judged deformed. Yet they are powerful and passionate figures. But the power and spirit reside in the appearance of a formal whole that cannot be broken up

19. Hans Leinberger, St. James, ca. 1520 (Munich,
Bayrisches Nationalmuseum)

Compare this with the seated figure of St. Mark by Fra Bartolommeo (Fig. 8) from
the same decade. In the St. Mark, the impression is determined by the great plastic
motifs; in the above figure, where the limbs are less clearly differentiated, it is determined by the over-all turmoil of forms.

into its components of body and clothing. It is precisely for this reason that the degree to which natural form has been preserved is of minor importance.

20. Lukas Cranach the Elder, Adam, 1528 (Florence, Uffizi)

5. In his youth, Dürer made a drawing of some soft cushions whose creases, despite their precise form, seem to change before our eyes. We might regard this as youthful playfulness; but Dürer's intentions were serious, and the drawing is a characteristic expression of the German concept of form. It would be difficult to find an Italian equivalent. When, later, the mature Dürer made his studies of draperies and of parts of the body with complete devotion to the plastic facts, his attitude was unchanged. In spite of everything, his drawings for the Heller Altarpiece are basically different from Italian drawings precisely because of that addition of a semblance of movement, or rather because of the conviction that an essential element lies in the contact between forms, in the way they are interconnected and intertwined. The apparently stiff and calm folds of an apostle's cloak quiver more than the most wildly fluttering Italian drapery; and the way in which the toes of a foot (whose form is fully and objectively fixed) are coiled within one another produces for the spectator a suggestion of movement for which an Italian would have never striven.

21. Lukas Cranach the Elder, Portrait of Dr. Scheuring, 1529 (Brussels, Museum)

This attitude has most important consequences for the interpretation of the organic forms of the head and body. The plastic character of the body in Italian art cannot be disassociated from the clear separation of parts; equally, the quality in a head which we call plastic is again the sharp separation of the forms, the way eye, nose, and cheek are distinctly set off from one another.

The sixteenth-century German artists also took up the representation of independent parts, but were unable to reconcile themselves to it fully because of a strong conflicting tradition. Even Dürer adhered to this tradition. Compared with Italian drawings, the forms of Dürer's nudes are more fluidly connected; and his heads, despite decided separation of details, generally retain an entwinement of forms that immediately marks him as a German. However, we become acquainted with the truly national style in the work of Cranach and Baldung. Their figures also have punctuating accents, which makes them strikingly different from the less punctuated bodies by Schongauer or Riemenschneider; yet what a close relationship exists between Cranach's figure of Adam of 1528 (Fig. 20) and Riemenschneider's Adam (Figs. 30, 31), created a generation earlier! Here we can see the evenness of an uninterrupted formal development; at the same time, we are all the more aware of the plastic and divisive interpretation in a drawing like Dürer's Adam of 1504. This work stemmed from his first reaction to Italian form; later he, too, sought a different equation between new and old.

The German flow of forms can be most immediately. experienced, however, in Baldung's female nudes (Fig. 59). Without renouncing dcfinitc form, Baldung makes us experience the image of female nudity mainly as a powerful undulation. He was also concerned with plastic values; but who would think of caesurae when looking at this compelling all-inclusive movement? That the reigning impression is not determined by the fullness of the flesh is proved by Cranach's later works, where a similar and completely un-Italian effect was obtained with delicately thin figures.

The same Cranach can also represent German portraiture with the magnificent head of Dr. Scheuring (Fig. 21). Certainly a feeling for plasticity pervades the work, which is unmistakably different from a fifteenth-century portrait; however, the distinctive feature of its style lies in the fluid movement of form, whose essential trait is the interweaving of serpentine curves rather than their cool juxtaposition. There are differences in degree: Dürer's work also contains movement, but it is often stiffened by the plastic demands made on the figures. We find movement particularly in his drawings and, in the portrait of his mother done in 1514, it is present in its most developed form.

4.   German Architecture

The Germans have to be content with the fact that their great masters, in whom they hail the "new life," felt at ease in "late Gothic" interiors. If we wish to form an idea of the architectural environment in which there developed the art of a Dürer, a Peter Vischer, of a Grünewald and a Backofen, of the buildings considered modern at the time, then we must think of the Mauthalle in Nuremberg or the Exchange in Freiburg, of town halls like those in Basel and Ensisheim, and of an ecclesiastical example like the Marienkirche in Halle. In just such a church, which belongs to the third decade of the sixteenth century, we are aware of a close tie with buildings constructed fifty years earlier. The choir of the Church of St. Lawrence in Nuremberg is so akin in its basic feeling that we feel sure it was still in style in the later period, even if it would no longer have been repeated literally. In any case, Veit Stoss sensed no stylistic incongruity when he hung his rose garland on the vaults of St. Lawrence's; and Dürer surely felt at home in his "Gothic" house near the *Tiergärtnertor.* The interior in his engraving of St. Jerome does not represent a romantic old-fashioned house but reflects the life of Dürer's time. But now the unexpected happens: even when Dürer, as a tectonic artist, used foreign forms, he thought it unnecessary to break with tradition. To him, there was more than one way of doing things, and *each* had its beauty. He did not consider the new Italian style incompatible with traditional Gothic; it was one more type of beauty. Thus the invasion of Italian motifs in the work of Burgkmair or Altdorfer does not denote a crisis. Altdorfer, whose work so strongly expresses certain traits of the German imagination, surprises us by the ease with which he accepted the foreign style.

This ready acceptance was possible only because the Italian Renaissance could dovetail with so much that already existed in the so-called late Gothic style. Rigid verticality had been shattered, and an agreement had been reached with horizontality; there was a feeling for spread out and widened space, and finally (the only point pertinent to the present discussion), volume and wall surface again had a say. But in contradistinction to Italian architecture, there were still no well-defined planes and no precise self-contained cubic proportions; interest was riveted on the movement of the undefined, and only here and there did clearly delimited form crystallize.

The Italian Renaissance gained a foothold in the North to the degree that planimetric and stereometric forms were valued for themselves and thus had meaning as self-sufficient entities. However, this occurred only conditionally. There is more of it in painting than in architecture. In general, we can say that while German classic architecture was not behind the times, it would look different if it had possessed a Dürer. However, it was not accidental that such a man was lacking: In the northern Renaissance, architecture *could* not play the leading role it did in Italy.

1. *Space*. Altdorfer's painting (Fig. 22), "The Birth of the Virgin" (Munich), characterizes well the fundamental difference between the German and Italian conceptions of space. Here, space is undefined and in motion. An immense garland of angels twines around the piers and cuts across the divisions between nave and aisles. It is a horizontal movement, and there is no Gothic upward *élan*. Yet it would be absurd to imagine a basilica by Brunelleschi interpreted in this way. With Brunelleschi, all forms are defined and distinct; in Altdorfer's interior, the nave and aisles flow into one another and, what is more, a rotating, whirling movement throws the entire space into turmoil.

The church's ground plan remains intentionally unclear; the painting compensates for the completeness of the diverse views offered to the spectator wandering on the spot by transforming finite into infinite form. Of course, something entirely different is meant when a complicated interior like Bramante's St. Peter's is called unsurveyable: with all the overlapping of parts, it can still be understood in its totality, and the visitor always knows exactly where he is. In Altdorfer's painting, the boundaries of the space are kept inconspicuous.

Surely Altdorfer intended this interior as a completely modern one (the form of the piers is modern); but, basically, the spatial conception is no different from that expressed in late Gothic architecture. Late Gothic hall churches must be understood in the same way. Although the motif of a large hall does bear some comparison with Italian interiors, its effect remains fundamentally different, since the spatial content is not contained within distinct limits.

With the Church of St. Michael in Munich, the change to the Italian style seems to have been completed. It was, in fact, the first large interior in Germany to be patterned after an Italian model. Its walls enclose, in a perfectly clear way, a unified barrel-vaulted space; yet the connection with tradition is unmistakable. This connection lies in the fact that its spatial proportions, in intentional deviation from the Italian model, produce an effect of movement and becoming, rather than one of static completeness. Despite its surveyability, the German building avoids plastic definition and retains because of that a somewhat intangible quality. That this is not an arbitrary interpretation is proved by the handling of the individual parts: the barrel vault does not rest on the wall as a self-enclosed half cylinder; but, instead, the verticality of the wall continues slightly into the vaulting. Thus, despite the cornice, the transition from wall to ceiling remains indeterminate.

When we turn from religious to secular interiors, we see even more easily the contrast between stressed and unstressed proportions. Life would be most painful in the majority of these northern rooms if we had to conceive of them as cubic entities of precise proportions and could not experience them with reference to movement. We may call it what we will: Whether we speak of an "intangible meshing" in the space, or its "painterly" character, there is something that fills every corner of these rooms and halls, and animates them. Because of this, we are not disturbed by irregular ground plans and too-low ceilings. This effect does not depend only on the furniture; more important is the treatment of wall and ceiling as active elements. Then, if something hangs or dangles into the space—a chandelier or a gourd—it merges quite naturally with the over-all movement. This objective-painterly character must be understood before we can understand the light that fills the space as movement. Again we must cite Dürer's engraving of St. Jerome as a typical example.

Late Gothic churches should be thought of as crowded with ecclesiastical furniture, figures, memorial plaques, etc., as they were

22. Albrecht Altdorfer, Birth of the Virgin (Munich, Alte Pinakothek)

intended to be seen. The piers lose nothing if such "ivy" clings to them, no more than trees in the forest do. Even the colossal structure of the infinitely popular Sacrament House by Adam Krafft leans on a pier like a parasite. A certain purification took place during the sixteenth century, but these habits survived the change in style. We can see this in secular architecture, where more examples of interior furnishings have been preserved than in the churches: Even pieces of furniture with Italianate forms cling so tightly to the wall that only in rare cases can we speak of them as "mobilia."[1] The "Swiss buffet"

---

[1] In the original, this is an untranslatable play on words: *"von Möbeln als mobilia sprechen kann."* [Tr.]

23. Munich,   (After Domenico
Frauenkirche   Quaglio, 1811)

is built into the room as something dependent-independent, like a
creeping plant, even at the most southerly borders of the German
cultural domain. The buffet lives only through its connection with
the whole room; if taken out and put on its own, it will collapse. This
is in complete opposition to plastically and independently conceived
Italian furniture.

2. *Exterior*. It would appear risky to deny the plastic character
of German architectural exteriors, since structural masses are of necessity delimited and are, moreover, sometimes seen in isolation. Without adhering strictly to the letter, we should clearly understand that
a different bodily response is demanded and evoked by Italian Renaissance architecture from that which we experience before contemporary German buildings. We refer once more to examples previously
cited: We comprehend the Frauenkirche in Munich (Fig. 23) not as
a precise form but in terms of a general impression of mass. And although the Mauthalle in Nuremberg (Fig. 24) is easier to survey, the
spectator never achieves that penetration of form for which "construc-

24. Nuremberg, Mauthalle, ca. 1500 (The openings in the wall are of recent date.)

tion according to proportion" is an absolute prerequisite; and there too he can gain only an approximate idea of the volume. However, the building does not suffer as a result, since exact proportions are not essential to it.

If we consider the frequency with which a high choir was patched onto a lower older building, resulting in an ugly, hump-like shape (for example, St. Lawrence's in Nuremberg), we will find that here, too, it is not a sufficient explanation to say that the emphasis was on interior effect. We will understand the procedure only if we realize that these buildings were not intended to be interpreted as three-dimensional solids, or at least not to the degree natural in Italy.

These projecting hump-like structures are not at all limited to additions to buildings (where one side of the structure was already fixed); houses with projecting stories lead to images that are similarly unbearable when seen in organic terms. As a form arising out of necessity, this type of house, at one time, was probably to be found everywhere; but German architecture was still using it in the six-teenth century—and with high artistic intentions (for example, the former Guild Hall of the Butchers in Hildesheim).

If we limit our scope to regular three-dimensional forms—which, after all, are in the majority—we will find that there, too, the German impulse toward movement continually blocked acceptance of Italian definiteness of proportion. The important factor for the Germans is what *happens* in a solid, not what it *is*. This is an epigrammatic ex-pression, since something also "happens" in the serene Italian archi-tecture; but it characterizes a distinction between North and South that never completely disappears. Even the new Town Hall of Roth-enburg, which is considered to be completely in the Italianate Renais-sance style, has little Italian distinctness of volume and much of the late Gothic Mauthalle in Nuremberg.

3. *Surface and detail.* Exactly the same attitude prevailed with regard to surface proportions. Wall surface was appreciated in the late Gothic style; but when decoration covers this surface, the interest is centered on the rhythm of the movement in this decoration and not on the proportions of well-defined planes. The image of a wall over-grown with ivy repeatedly comes to mind, the specific form of the wall being subordinated to these elements animating the wall. It was noted above that even in an decidedly Italianate structure like the Ott-Heinrich façade at Heidelberg Castle, the surface panels between the articulating supports have little importance. In Italy, they would have received the greatest emphasis; here, the predominant impres-sion is of a general movement rippling over the wall. In German Renaissance façades, this was standard practice. Calculation of pro-portions did exist, but was secondary.

The late Gothic cupboard (Fig. 25) displays a readiness to grant importance to the plane—it has smooth walls with sunken panels

25. Late Gothic Cupboard, ca. 1500
(Munich, Nationalmuseum)

The contrast between stressed and unstressed surface proportions becomes clear when
the above is compared with Fig. 7. The concomitant difference—the German aversion
to articulated organization—is treated in Chapter III.

filled with ornament. But nowhere is it a question of precise proportion; and this very ornament creates uncertainty about the proportions of the sunken panels, since it does not coincide with the given form. Only Peter Flötner, out of a new appreciation of the beauty of proportion, treated exteriors in such a way that, by means of ornament, the beauty of the well-defined panel is acknowledged and made prominent. Hence, Peter Flötner is considered the "classicist" among German architects and was quickly neglected by popular taste.

The bounded plane was not accepted, even when it seemed to have come about of itself. What could be more natural in a gable façade than to clearly separate the triangular gable as a self-contained form from the rectangular understructure? This was not done. Just as in late Gothic architecture, where gable decoration can be understood only in connection with the entire wall and is not separated from the wall by a horizontal cornice, so in the following period it remains a characteristic of the German style that the gable is not set off from the understructure as a distinct part but grows out from it. (Even in St. Michael's in Munich, where the cornices are strongly stressed, everything was done to keep the gable from achieving independence.)

This lack of separation or—to express it positively—this need for an over-all undifferentiated movement of masses, also conditions the relationship between support and vaulting and has occasionally led to the most singular results in the formation of the parts. We can imagine nothing more incomprehensible to the Italian taste than those vault supports in the Castle of Meissen; there, entirely heterogeneous forms shoot upward in bundles and merge with the ceiling, where the single ribs are lost in an indeterminate way. The sixteenth century no longer solved the problem in *this* fashion, but the motif of supports that suddenly disappear in the vault was still used fifty years later in the Marienkirche in Halle (ca. 1530). Although the German imagination reconciled itself to the column, it seems to have found it particularly hard in this respect to replace indefinite by definite form. In the Old Lusthaus in Stuttgart, the columns of the hall in their function still visibly overlap the beginning of the vault; and, in any case, during the entire German Renaissance the column retained a connection with the wall that prevented the emergence of the disengaged beauty of the Italian column. We shall return to this later.

4. *Site.* As if a fear of losing contact with the fundamentals of life had restrained the creative imagination from increasing the independence of single forms, so the imagination also clung on a large scale to the externally given conditions of the site and was content therewith.

The character of the German *Gasse,* or lane, is essentially conditioned by the great number of dependent houses, none of which is self-sufficient and each of which can only exist by leaning on its neighbor. Of course, such houses are also found in Renaissance cities of Italy, but there they impress us as having arisen out of necessity. In any event, when one of these is built on a larger scale, it tends to present itself as an independent structure. In Germany, this is not the case. Even a monumental building tolerates dependence. Although there are, of course, examples of detached architecture, the reigning spirit is generally one of cohesion, which recognized no decrease in value when even a towering building is dependent on and conditioned by others. Monumentality then lies in the entire compact group of buildings. We can again refer to the Guild Hall in Hildesheim, which was certainly intended to be grand and dignified but the effect of which is distorted into caricature when the support of a similar neighboring house is removed (as has actually been done).

The German house grows in accordance with the possibilities inherent in its site. It carries its laws of form only partly within itself. A little square opens up, or the street widens somewhat—a bay that juts into the open space is promptly added to a house. We are immediately aware of a relationship in which the favorable and unfavorable elements of a given site act as form-producing and form-inhibiting factors. Even monumental architecture can share in this interrelated growth of building and surroundings. The Town Hall of Rothenburg is a famous example. Situated on rising ground, it makes no attempt to deny the conditions of a site that hindered unified design; on the contrary, it courageously accepts these external circumstances, achieving a kind of naturalness that would never have been appreciated in Italy. Thus is explained an asymmetrical organization in which one bay projects into the square and the staircase turret is off-center. Surely, this building is not regulated by its own laws of organization alone but receives them in part from the outside; nevertheless, we do not feel this dependency to be an impairment of its vitality.

5. Contour

If further confirmation of the plastic focus of Italian art were necessary, we could cite Alberti's requirement that the painter should model a head first before painting it on a two-dimensional surface. Only by modeling a form can the artist be certain of having grasped its full plastic value. This is a fundamental statement in favor of the tangible facts as the true essential. It is almost surprising that Leonardo did not repeat this requirement; but, to him, the plastic concept of form was already self-evident.

The correlate of plastic interpretation is line in its function as contour. Therefore, we may also speak of linear style (in the sense of a contouring style) in the place of plastic style. Here, the value of line lies first in the absolutely clear indication of limits. This concept is, of course, valid not only for painting but for all the pictorial arts. It is a question of bounded form everywhere, and everywhere the task is the same, namely, the unequivocally clear representation of precise entities. When line in Italian art is said to be of particular simplicity and tranquility, what is being put into words is a mood that has nothing to do with plasticity as such. However, it is evident that a simple straightforward contour can be more effective in conferring form than a complicated and agitated line. Alberti and Leonardo were of the same opinion concerning the fundamental importance of the contour (inner forms also have their contours): drawing is outlining (circumscriptio). Although all objects are silhouetted in some way, the conception of the contour as a guiding line is something special.

The emphasis on contour determined the physiognomy of the Italian Renaissance from the outset. The burden of explaining form was placed on the contour, which at the same time was made rhyth-

26. Domenico Ghirlandaio, Giovanna Tornbuoni. Drawing
(London, British Museum)

mic, and could thus appear self-sufficient. A head by Ghirlandaio
(Fig. 26) rests within its contour as within a golden ring; the line defines the form and yet has a melody of its own. When the grand spirit
of the sixteenth century begins to use this language of contour, we
witness the extremely magnificent spectacle of clearer and clearer
delineation of form joined with increasingly significant rhythmic
motifs. As if of itself, line of the greatest clarity seems to have also
become line of a self-contained beauty. The significance of this art-
historical phenomenon is not diminished by the fact that new fascination was soon felt in Italy for the departure from the ideal of per-

27. Albrecht Dürer, Adam and Eve. Drawing, 1504
(Pierpont Morgan Library)

fectly clear drawing, and that Correggio, in the middle of the High
Renaissance, began to develop contour in opposition to form.

In the North, things were entirely different. Here too, it is true,
the sixteenth century saw the ripening desire to give the outline

greater emphasis and meaning; but this desire found opposition in a tradition of interlaced line and hostility to contour. The new style could not and would not counteract this tradition. The opposing tendencies interpenetrated, and classic drawing in Germany thus acquired an essentially different aspect than in Italy.

Let us not deceive ourselves. It is true that Dürer's 1504 drawing (Fig. 27) for his engraving of Adam and Eve looks very Italian: the expressive contours of the figures reveal the entire motif, and the rhythmically enclosed silhouettes are easily apprehended. But how isolated this style is in German art! It is admirable that Dürer was able to achieve—in his first attempt, so to speak—such a pure solution to the new problem; and his example was not without sequel. But how little the copious production of the period resembles this drawing, and how little of Dürer's own work is in the same vein!

We repeat: The tradition was one of interlaced line and hostility to contour. Let us consider Schongauer as the representative of pre-Düreresque drawing. Schongauer's work—for example, his "Death of the Virgin"—displays an interweaving of line that is completely foreign to Italian graphic art. We do not wish to underestimate the effect of his more crinkly stroke, which is advantageous to the spectacle of movement; but more important is the fact that line is not used as a leading and objectively conditioned contour. Even in the single figure of the Virgin in his "Annunciation" (Fig. 80), the lily gnaws into the garment in such a way that we immediately become aware of the disregard for silhouette. These characteristics have a long history in northern art. The unstressed contour is poor in expression. Compared with Masaccio, the figures of Adam and Eve in the Ghent Altarpiece have completely accidental contours. And, while the contour of Uccello's horse for the equestrian figure in the Florentine Duomo seems to be altogether inevitable, in Germany even Burgkmair's equestrian figure of Emperor Maximilian (in a woodcut of 1508) contains traits that prevent us from speaking of an accentuated autonomous contour. We cannot call this backwardness: the Germans shied away from an isolating contour style because it was a threat to the essential merging of forms, that mysterious coherence of the whole that also had existed long before Schongauer.

Nevertheless, the new interest in the figure gave rise to a new

interest in contour in the North as well. But the contour did not affect
the whole of drawing; along with pronounced silhouetting, incidental contour always held its ground. A consistent use of contour has a
chilling effect on the Germans. Certainly, we can say that silhouettes
in Italian paintings are not all uniformly stressed; but what does that
mean when compared to the proportions of accentuated and unac-
centuated lines in German art! Dürer knew well what he was doing
when he placed the figures of Adam and Eve in the engraving in
front of a "painterly" woodland background. In the large painted
nudes that were to follow, the light bodies are finally silhouetted
against a pure black ground, which surely contributes to an Italian
effect; but this effect is counterbalanced by other elements. We ob-
serve that the contour is not closed in a uniformly confining ring and
that it is knotted with the inner forms in an entirely different way
from that found in Italian art. It is the same with Cranach's later
figures on black backgrounds; and it is highly characteristic that even
the presentation of the complete figure was not considered important.
The truly decisive examples of German drawing, however, should be
sought in those works where, in *one* place in the picture, the contour
stands out purely and radiantly from a sphere of limited clarity, i.e.,
of more accidental line. The pointing arm of St. John in the Isenheim "Crucifixion" is an example of this kind: the figure as a whole
is not conceived as a silhouette figure in the Italian sense, but only
this one part. From this stems the figure's tremendous impact. However, entire figures are also presented as both silhouette and non-
silhouette figures, as in Baldung's woodcut of "The Fall of Man."

The tradition of intertwined form persisted in the North, even
with the presence of the stressed contour. To be sure, the plastic indistinctness of the primitives had to give way; and in Dürer's woodcuts of the Small Passion, the contours are more tangible than
before. Nonetheless, the figures remain so deeply embedded in a
total unity that, by contrast, any Italian work seems to have an
isolating contour style. Marcantonio's copies of Dürer's prints impress us as strange, because the Italian, according to national custom,
made the contours so pronounced. He copies the details with great
exactitude, yet did not understand the style. To the Germans, an
essential beauty resides in the fact that the whole is a web of lines in
which even the most expressive single contour remains interwoven.

28. Hans Baldung,
The Fall of Man, 1519

Such hypotheses also explain the German predilection for white line drawings and woodcuts since a play of line independent of the form is, so to speak, automatically produced in them, even when the figures are absolutely clear. (See Fig. 29.)

If light and shadow are introduced, the "painterly" effect is even more easily achieved. These elements unite in a compelling over-all movement precisely when the shadows are not dependent on the figures and not restricted to an objective statement. What would Dürer's woodcuts of the Small Passion be (to stay with the previous example) without the completely irrational scattering of lights and darks! We shall return to this later. For the moment, we shall say only that in this procedure, too, Dürer is linked with earlier masters like Schongauer, while, on the other hand, he prepares the way for Rembrandt. In Italian classic art, the use of light was first of all a matter of plastic clarity; and if artists deviated from this concept, it was in search of an increased attractiveness that has a different meaning from the natural irrationality of the Germans.

The same can be said of the use of color. The tapestry-like organization of color in the early multipartite folding altarpieces was simplified in the altar paintings of the sixteenth century in the direction of stronger single effects and more distinct objective meaning. However, color preserved its individual life, independent of form.

This autonomous life completely parallels the effects in drawing and, in the degree found here, is foreign to Italian art.

We cannot overestimate the importance for sculpture of this contrast between an accentuated, form-saturated, and rhythmically closed contour and a type of drawing that stresses the silhouette only sporadically and aims at an interplay of lines. While paintings are unambiguous, sculptured figures can be viewed in different ways; and current illustrations indicate that a common opinion as to which is the correct way has not yet been achieved. This much is certain: one of the most essential attributes of classic art in Italy is that even the free-standing figure was intended to have one completely definite silhouette. Without detriment to the possibility of observing the three-dimensional form from all sides, the front view forcibly asserts itself as the main view. In this view the form-explaining contour is suddenly closed in a melodious line; and the spectator can gain great pleasure by returning repeatedly from the secondary views to the principal view, which has acquired a quality of inevitability. This style was not developed consistently until the High Renaissance, although it had always existed in latent form, and highly gifted artists had occasionally anticipated purely classic solutions. To this group belongs Donatello's "David" (Fig. 9). If we ask why such a figure could not have been created in the North, we again hit upon the psychological fact that, there, the contour was not the natural mode of interpretation. As in painting, the contour in German sculpture retains a certain hovering and indefinite quality. We cannot speak of intentional clarity and beauty of silhouette in the figures even though they are conceived as single-plane figures and should not be photographed from an angle (a mistake that is often made). The most refined works—such as Tilman Riemenschneider's "Adam," which decidedly needs to be viewed from the front—are precisely those that are not firmly established within a definite and tangible contour and retain something fluctuating in their appearance. (See Figs. 30 and 31.)

The sixteenth century brought a change. But strict contour style in the Italian sense was still the exception. Vischer's figures of knights from the tomb of Emperor Maximilian in Innsbruck were no doubt planned with an eye for contour. (What a pity that not a single photograph brings these merits to the fore!) The same holds true for

29. Urs Graf, Family of Satyrs. Reverse Woodcut, 1520

Adolf Daucher's Lamentation group in Augsburg. But along with these, painterly flickering sculpture like the "Annunciation in the Rose Garland" (Nuremberg, St. Lawrence's) by the aged Veit Stoss was still possible—not because people wanted the old man to have his way and speak once more in the style of a bygone time, but because the "painterly" style fully belonged among the living possessions of the present. Indeed only then were the ultimate consequences of its fifteenth-century development manifested. The German Renaissance was unable to break with tradition but, instead, had to develop it further. We can see the modern painterly style in the sculpture of

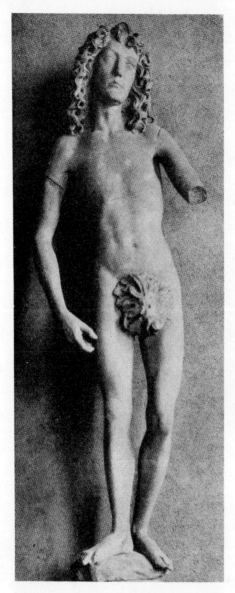

30. Tilman Riemenschneider, Adam 1494
(Würzburg, Museum)
Approximately correct photograph.

31. Tilman Riemenschneider
Same figure as in Fig. 30
Incorrect photograph

the great Backofen, a man of the new generation. Backofen's work, in contrast to that of Veit Stoss, excels in the magnificent certainty of the objective appearance. Yet Backofen never renounced the spell of over-all movement that dominates and pervades every detail. His forms have definite contours, but the painterly continuity is never interrupted. We have to admit that a work like the Gemmingen Tomb (Fig. 32) must have corresponded to the German formal instincts more than Italianizing classicism did. Nevertheless, from an historical viewpoint, we should not underestimate the significance that lay precisely in the one-sidedness of such classicism; nor can we judge the short-lived phenomenon of "pure" plastic form in Germany as a mere developmental by-product. There was at that time, too, both a genuine and a false classicism; and in the last analysis, a hidden relationship links the bishops of the Gemmingen tomb to the knights from the tomb of Emperor Maximilian.

32. Hans Backofen, Tomb of Archbishop Uriel von Gemmingen (died 1514)
(Mainz, Cathedral)

The composition already takes into account the contrast between vacant and filled areas. The upright form of the whole is interrupted by the horizontality of the middle void.   The definite form of the arch blends into the indefinite form of the canopy.

II. REGULARITY AND ORDER

ALL ART, AS THE WORK OF MAN, is differentiated from nature by a conformity to laws which, while apparent in individual natural products (although never in pure form), is at all events lacking in nature as a whole. Against nature's arbitrariness, we set the order of art. Wherever trees stand in a straight row, there human hands have been at work; the freely growing wood knows no rules. Civilized man needs to establish himself in the world in orderly fashion—we could not live without straight lines and right angles.

But the other realm, the realm that is free and not subject to rules is, after all, not a bad thing either. Besides geometric order, there is free form which cannot be apprehended, it is true, in terms of laws, but which nevertheless is not the same as formlessness. Both the architectonic column and the natural tree have their beauty; but in the one it is the beauty of a life restrained by tectonic laws, in the other the beauty of free organic life.

The tastes of nations are divided with respect to the preference for either severe or free form. It is not that they one-sidedly recognize only one of the two kinds of beauty: it is simply a question of the relative value assigned to each. When we think of Italy, we see clearly that the principle of tectonic regularity predominated there to the same degree that the principle of free rhythmicality did in the North. The South read the column into the tree, the North the tree into the column. Thus, architecture was the leading art in Italy; and it can also be said that the painters of the Renaissance saw everything *sub specie architecturae.*

Although we hold architecture in general to be the art of rule and order, we can nevertheless draw a distinction between one rule and another. During the Italian Renaissance, the notion of rule was realized so decisively and consistently that, in comparison, the German concept of form appears loose and arbitrary. We gather from this clear-cut adherence to rule that the Italians found it to be not a limitation of their freedom but, on the contrary, a manifestation of a wholly free and natural life. For the Germans, some trace of wilfulness, some trace of broken rules must always remain if they are to believe in the freedom of existence; and a consistent clinging to laws easily has an artificial effect. In Italy, on the other hand, the most severe form is at the same time the most vital. As for architecture, the regularity of the ground plan finds its natural concomitant in the regularity of the sequence of forms. Symmetry is prized as the natural basis for all invention of form; and, going beyond this symmetry, a feeling for regularity in the diversified individual proportions and formal motifs of an organism has been developed, guaranteeing the greatest formal unity. The same holds true for painting. Italy has produced an abundance of paintings designed from a purely tectonic viewpoint, with emphasis on the central axis and symmetrical treatment of the two sides. The Germans are barely able to accept this principle even in tranquil groups of figures and still less in lively historical scenes. Raphael, however, could unhesitatingly make use of the pattern in both his "School of Athens" and the highly dramatic "Expulsion of Heliodorus." These works are of course large murals; but the same principle was also readily applied to the smallest paintings. Such obedience to rule does not have the unnatural quality it does in Germany. In atectonic compositions, however, other principles of harmony are in force, resulting in a picture equally rulebound, although in a different way. Indeed, even the individual body and individual head as formal entities are also subject to the principles of rule and order. The structure of the human body has some inherent kinship with architecture, and this architectonic quality can be intensified by emphasizing the body's geometric system; but the Renaissance was particularly concerned with showing that the totality of the different forms composing the body also is subject to certain laws. We may then speak of the harmony of forms, and rightly so; but the specific point consists in the *strict* harmony which unites the forms, a harmony to which the Italians early proved themselves receptive. Alberti's doctrine, characterizing perfection as a harmony *based on rule* (certa *cum ratione* concinnitas), points in the same direction. Needless to say, Antiquity was both teacher and model.

The sixteenth century was a period of heightened need for stricter order in the North as well. The horizontal and the vertical became the leading directions in pictorial art. The central axis and the balance of the sides were emphasized more strongly. The Germans, too, occasionally engaged in tectonic design. However, structure never attained Italian strictness; and the application of the concept of order seems to have been enevitably accompanied by a desire for a relaxation of order. Only when the rules were fully understood did divergence from them afford true joy to the imagination. Certain works by Altdorfer are freer than any produced before his time.

We cannot consider it a deficiency that the North has never adhered strictly to rules and frequently even treated them lightly; rather, this expresses a distinct and positive basic attitude indicative of the entire German relationship to nature. Germans do not *believe* in the absolute value of rules but perceive a streak of irrationality in all living things. This feeling for an irrationality that simply cannot be expressed in stable forms already conditions the style of the German primitives, a style that may appear particularly "formless" in comparision with Italian art. The great generation of sixteenth-century artists valued rules more highly than did their predecessors; yet, for it too, there was evidently a remainder that could not be carried over into the sphere of lucid order.

We encounter here, as was said above, fundamental differences in the conception of nature. Nothing is more indicative than Leonardo's advice to artists in his "Trattato della pittura" to pay attention to the regular organization of branches of trees—the yearly shoots follow one another in concentric semicircles. A German could scarcely have said that. This observation did not become a formula for Italian painters; yet nowhere but in German painting do we encounter that pleasure in the self-assertive spreading of branches that became the vehicle of a very large part of German formal imagination. In Italy, every twig and every tuft of grass is lined up in more regular fashion, and the "accidental" entwining of plants in Dürer's "Great Piece of Turf" can perhaps be appreciated fully only by German eyes. For the North, the distinctive feature of a flock of birds or a group of clouds has been, from early times onward, the intangible free rhythm; and the forms of flowing water, or the grain in wood, always retain something irrational in their movement. In Italy, these phenomena are always instinctively rationalized.

The difference appears most clearly in the realm of ornamental forms. What a wonder of free rhythmical motion is the crown of thorns of the crucified Christ in the Isenheim Altarpiece! It is the quintessence of the German decorative spirit of the grand style. Italian artists chose to see in the crown of thorns little more than an orderly braid.

Wherever the North also emphasizes the regular and ordered aspects of phenomena, a closeness to Italy naturally results. Yet it is strange that Dürer was so cautious in relation to Italian ornament: his drawings for the margins of the Prayer-Book of Emperor Maximilian are still fundamentally German, although they would be inexplicable without Italian models.

In the last analysis, the contrast can be summed up in the two concepts of the tectonic and the vegetative. However, to interpret this contrast as an "either-or" would lead at once to erroneous results. We can only conclude this much from the above-mentioned examples: Italians tend to stylize their ornament in a tectonic direction to the same degree that Germans, bursting all tectonic bonds, need to give vent to their delight in the spiral and, hence, in the free forms of the tendril and branch. Dürer's designs for mural decorations of the Nuremberg Town Hall are typical.

Architecture

It has been observed that the medieval castle in Italy usually has a regular basic form, an octagon or a square, while the German castle grows in regular-irregular fashion out of the given configuration of the site, which the Germans, with "hunter-like adaptability" (Klaiber) know how to use to advantage. This contrast is even more characteristic of the Renaissance. It was still possible in Florence for the Palazzo della Signoria to be erected with an irregular ground plan, despite the architect's opposition; but, during the Renaissance, such a compromise would no longer have been acceptable. The regular ground plan was taken for granted, not only in monumental buildings, but also in private houses; and this means, in addition, that regularity was also required of the shape of the individual room and of the disposition of all the rooms. In the North, on the other hand, even in the sixteenth century, no one minded if the ground plan of a house or a room was irregular. The regular was only *one* form of life, perhaps the more highly valued, but by no means the inevitable one. Even in the monumental structure of a Renaissance town hall, for example, an irregular entrance hall was not disconcerting. However, it is easy to imagine that wherever regularity did materialize under these circumstances, it could appear in an ideally heightened splendor.

The need to divest the site of its accidental character and to give value and dignity to the terrain by a clearly ordered architectural arrangement is universal in Italy. Even today, we can see how a place of rural enjoyment, the garden in front of a mountain inn or the like, is endowed by modest means with distinctive architectural form. A northerner, in the same place, would have been thoroughly content with untamed nature. Thus, the architectonic garden arose in Italy; and there, in the planning of cities, the Antique principles of regular form were again considered with aesthetic awareness. A symmetrical *piazza* was the pride of a city; and the desire to make the walls around the square uniform if they presented a variegated appearance was universal. Michelangelo is said to have proposed surrounding the Piazza della Signoria on all sides with the portico motif of the Loggia dei Lanzi; and there exists a plan by Peruzzi to make the Campo in Siena uniform.

No one will claim that regularity of *sequence* is a motif exclusive to Italy. Even rows of windows and the like are found everywhere; but it is remarkable how this kind of order stands out on the very entry into an Italian city. The North has regular sequence in its church windows; but in monumental civic structures no stress is laid on regularity, and in private buildings it is almost entirely absent. It is usually said that the northerner built from the inside out and made the disposition of windows dependent on their purpose; but this explanation disregards the positive element of joy in free rhythm. Strict order is also known to the North, but it is the exception; in the South it is the rule, and the principle asserts itself with greater vigor. The imposing and severe ranks of windows in Florentine and Roman palaces have, in fact, no equal. But even Venetian palaces must have seemed strangely rigid and restrained to German travelers of former times.

The characteristic southern *symmetry* results from the emphasis on the center. The entrance door is set in the middle of the façade and the rooms are grouped, wherever possible, along the central axis. This arrangement was customary in Italy—so customary that it was probably no longer associated with any special impression of solemnity. It was simply the form assumed by life. Asymmetrical groups of buildings, already rare in the fifteenth century, were no longer created at all in the sixteenth or only with an end to achieving a rural and informal effect. In the North, asymmetry was perpetuated, not merely as one possibility but as the favorite form, which was found compatible even with the goal of monumentality. An aura of the exceptional, the distinguished—even the sacred—must have clung to the purely symmetrical arrangement. But all along, people readily abandoned intended symmetry, even in church design! The identical towers of the Frauenkirche in Munich almost seem to react in protest to this abandonment.

In the final analysis, regularity was a problem of proportion. No part was to be left to free estimation; instead, everything had to appear inevitable and had to have that manifest order admired in ancient buildings. Alberti put it into words. His Palazzo Rucellai is the first step on the road that leads to Bramante.

The impression of *regulated proportionality* is essentially achieved through adherence to a precise and consistent relationship. Thus, for example, the proportions of window frames would match those of the wall panels to which they belonged; and the proportions of each panel would conform with those of the entire façade. Of course, this example covers only part of the problem. Along with two-dimensional proportions, three-dimensional proportions also have to be considered. Ultimately, the problem is contained in the demand for formal unity both in details and in the whole, in the requirement that a definite tonality be maintained throughout and that a totally heterogeneous shape not appear suddenly and, as something accidental, destroy the impression of regulated order. It is in these terms that we have to understand the precept in classic Italian architecture that a cupola over the crossing of a church had to be accompanied by a barrel-vaulted nave (and not by a flat-roofed one) and that the transept of that church had to have semicircular ends. Contrasting forms were not excluded; on the contrary, they were to assert themselves. But they had to be real contrasts, contrasts that complemented each other and were not merely different.

The quality of Italian architecture we designate regulated harmony has some of its roots in the features discussed above (still another aspect of the question will be considered in the next chapter). Many a German must have experienced this beauty as a liberation and believed themselves to be face to face with divine perfection. Let them not be deceived—this art, too, was nationally conditioned; and while it can make them happy for a short time, it can never become permanently and exclusively theirs. The Italian aesthetic is clearly connected with the feeling for well-defined form. It could have developed only in a world of purely plastic values, and only there can it be meaningful; in Germany, where plasticity always has to compromise with movement and indefiniteness, its sphere of influence is an essentially different one. Thus, even these values were of little concern to Germans of the sixteenth century.

In order to bring out this contrast clearly, we shall pass over contemporary "late Gothic" monuments and use for comparison a late sixteenth-century structure, the Town Hall of Rothenburg (ca. 1570), which is considered to be in the fully developed German-Italian Renaissance style (Fig 33).

Let us weigh in our minds how little the following features belong to the Renaissance in the Italian sense.

1. The New Town Hall forms a whole together with the Gothic portion, which, with its tower, is situated behind it. To be sure, this combination was not intentional but, rather, came about accidentally; it met no opposition, however, in the prevailing taste. In the original layout, a parallel wing had already existed there which, after a fire, was to be replaced in modern style. Thus, an aggregate of heterogeneous parts arose; but it need not be thought that the dissonance between old and new was viewed as an aesthetic sacrifice. Germany abounds in such cases. The Marktkirche in Halle, built around 1530, was placed between the spires of two older churches that had been torn down. It cannot be accidental that similar things practically never happened in Italy.

2. The staircase turret stands in the middle of the façade. However, we would be mistaken if we interpreted it as emphasis on the central axis. The turret marks the center only approximately, for the sides to its right and left are unequal. (Characteristically, the rusticated portico, placed in front of the building a hundred years later, does not continue this irregularity.) An Italian architect would have strongly resisted such asymmetry. Even a moderate-sized private building required a central portal—to say nothing of a monumental structure. Here, the intention was to give the building a livelier effect by means of that very asymmetry. In the late Gothic Mauthalle in Nuremberg (Fig. 24), the large structure on the roof is likewise pushed to one side; and the severe Renaissance style of the Town Hall of Emden did not prevent the portal from being moved away from the middle. We might explain the latter asymmetry as the result of consideration for a street passage; however, it was only in the North that such considerations were not regarded as disturbances of the artistic scheme. Purely symmetrical plans were occasionally realized, but they represented, as said above, only one among different possibilities. The corner bay of the Rothenberg Town Hall is solitary and asymmetrical, too, and clearly refers to the conditions of the site.

3. A related motif is the irregular sequence of windows. On the gable façade, groups of two and of four windows are placed next to each other; on the main façade, a single group of three windows is mixed altogether irrationally into the row of double windows. Strangely enough, this is not disturbing. Some higher rhythmical law must be acting as compensation. It is well known that windows were rarely spaced evenly in private buildings; we should also bear in mind that this freedom gave rise to extraordinarily vigorous effects, and that German streets lost a great deal when refined symmetrical façades gradually supplanted the bold rhythm of the older houses that had grown so naturally.

4. We cannot expect a structure built in this spirit to have consistent axes. The windows of the two main stories, it is true, do correspond; but on the gable side, the distribution in the gable is different from that in the wall below, and here again, the ground story differs in its organization from the upper stories. The place-

33. Rothenburg o.T., Town Hall

ment of the dormer windows on the roof is even more striking, since
the principle of distribution does not match that in the façade. The
problem was always handled in this way; indeed, in the early years
of the century the inconsistencies were much more violent, and were
appreciated not only in private houses but also in great monumental
structures. Among the illustrations at our disposal here, the Exchange in Freiburg (Fig. 6) provides an instructive comparison—the
ground floor has four arches, above which are the five large windows
of the main story. The latter, of course, cannot accord with the arches.
In addition, the roof introduces two new rhythms with its (restored)
dormer windows. This motif of dissonant organization is completely
contrary to the classic Italian concept of form; and an example like

34. Regensburg, Model of the "Schöne Maria"

the fifteenth-century Town Hall of Pesaro (with merely *one* change of rhythm) constitutes an exception for the Renaissance.

5. Another manifestation of the same turn of mind is the lack of concern for formal homogeneity in the whole. In Italy, this homogeneity plays a decisive role in the creation of the impression of total harmony. The same attributes enjoyed by Italians in the beautiful human body—analogy within contrast, symmetricality of organization along with differentiation of the parts—were carried over to architec-

35. Todi, Santa Maria della Consolazione

ture. It was first of all a matter of proportions—that is to say, of a fixed relationship prevailing throughout the whole. But it was also a morphological problem of a special kind: round and rectangular, cylindrical and prismatic forms had to be kept from jostling one another in an accidental, unplanned, or self-contradictory way unless it were a question of complementary contrasts. German art reveals a basically different attitude. Of course, it, too, did not desire disharmony; but the strict Italian harmony goes totally counter to an entirely free harmony whose nature is such that very different proportions and types of form are compatible in a single building. A group of buildings that would look like an aggregate of heterogeneous parts to eyes schooled in Italy can still appear to a German as a rhythmically united whole. The law of consistent proportions which August Thiersch derived from Italian architecture and laid down as a general law,[1] is not applicable to precisely the finest buildings of the German Renaissance; yet no one can deny their exciting rhythm. Thus, Thiersch's requirement of a homogeneity of formal characteristics is invalidated. Gradually, the North also became "harmonized"; but like Rothenburg, the town halls of Altenburg (Fig. 46) and Schweinfurt—all Renaissance buildings in the precise sense of the term—also contain formal dissonances that would have been unacceptable to Italian taste. But it is these very dissonances that make these town halls look so familiar and friendly to Germans. Even in the late façade of the Italianizing St. Michael's in Munich (Fig. 68), little attempt was made to seek beauty in a consistent harmony of the whole and its parts, although the principle is clearly evident in single forms.

We conclude with an example that fits better into the period under discussion: the model of the "Schöne Maria" church in Regensburg (ca. 1520), one of the most interesting expressions of the new style (Fig. 34). How little it conforms to the law of analogy: its semicircular chapels jut out of a polygonal choir; its onion-shaped cupolas, atop the spires, neighbor on a steep tent-shaped roof. These are contradictions that can be justified only within the German aesthetic. It would be wrong to regard them merely as expressions of an impure transitional taste, for they are deeply rooted in the national concept of form. We might cite as an Italian contrast the central structure of the Consolazione in Todi (Fig. 35). Here, everything goes together. The culminating cupola is prepared for from the beginning, and the opposing round and rectangular forms act as complementary contrasts. This is a High Renaissance work; but, as far as regularity and similarity of parts are concerned, the choir of the Florentine Duomo had already been conceived in a similar spirit.

6. We must briefly draw attention once more to the fact that German architecture submitted more readily than Italian architec-

---

[1] Durm's *Handbuch der Architektur* IV, first half. More accessible in Burckhardt's *Renaissance in Italien* (3rd and later editions).

ture to terrain and accidental circumstances. The irregular was not sought out, but neither was it avoided. The rising ground on which the Town Hall of Rothenburg was built could never have permitted perfect regularity of the structure. Similar examples occurred repeatedly, and apparently caused German architects no embarrassment. In Italy, irregularity was always something to be shunned.

Pictorial Art

1. When northerners see a great many Italian paintings exhibited together, as in the large museums, they are surprised over and over again at the large number of them that are composed according to tectonic laws and at the strictness with which these laws were enforced. They are less surprised to find iconic images of saints subjected to this pattern, although similar types of pictures are few in the North; but what seems remarkable to them is that the narrative painting is also symmetrically organized, that animated events can be depicted with the stressed central axis and the similarly composed sides that we find in architecture. To compose a painting of the Slaughter of the Innocents symmetrically runs counter to German instinct. Only a Romanistic mannerism, which can no longer claim originality in its conception of form, offers some analogy. The Germans are also acquainted with symmetrical organization, and it was precisely the sixteenth century that adopted the form with new strictness; but they always associate all tectonic order with the impression of the deliberate, the solemn, and the unusual. In any case, for them it is a form that does not happen of its own accord in living things. In the South, even natural gestures can be crystallized into geometric form without damage to the impression of life.

Symmetry, however, is only a single, and particularly obvious, kind of tectonic order. Tectonic order can be present in equal measure in a picture with merely one figure: for example, a painting of St. Sebastian. The figure of the saint with his column can keep so strictly to the middle of the picture and be so strictly placed on the middle axis of the panel that the internal connection between the figure and the form of the panel (which is in itself regular) cannot be overlooked. It is not that the figure is governed by the shape of the picture, but rather that the figure accommodates itself to it voluntarily. Just as the figure shares in the architectonic quality of the panel, the panel receives, in return, character and value.

And if, within the same connection between figure and panel, the elementary directions of the horizontal and vertical are dominant, again the principle of rectangularity is not imposed on the pictorial content from the outside but harmonizes freely with the regular structure of the panel.

This harmony, however, is even more far-reaching: in revealing only its own self, the picture refers at the same time to the frame. Thus, surface and enclosure seem to be there just for each other. Whether there be right angles, or the top of the picture be a semi-circle, or whether the whole painting be circular in shape, we feel that the relation between framing and framed elements is an inevitable one. It is self-evident that this closeness of one form to the other is continued within the picture. The result is a connection between figure and setting, as well as between figure and figure, which is divested of any accidental character. Even the individual parts of the figure—a hand, for example—are embedded in the picture in such a way that it seems impossible to displace them.

Any analysis of masterpieces of regulated order, such as Leonardo's "Last Supper" or Raphael's tapestries, will furnish examples of this kind of harmony.

Our mention of Raphael's tapestries leads us to the remarkable fact that both tectonic and non-tectonic composition can occur within the same style and in relation to the same task. The "Death of Ananias" is symmetrically composed, while the "Miraculous Draught of Fishes" is without geometric backbone. Titian's "Assunta" has the stressed middle axis, while in the "Murder of St. Peter Martyr," (Fig. 51) the same artist manages without it. In neither case can we speak of looser form, for, in both, an ordering principle of the strictest kind prevails; but the impression of regularity was sought essentially in the realm of similarity of forms (and contrast of forms). Tectonic order is only a particular kind of order.

We may next inquire as to where each system was applied and whether the procedures were, in principle, always the same. It is understandable that the feeling for formal harmony developed only

36. Leonardo da Vinci, The Last Supper. (After an engraving by Stang)

gradually to the height we admire in the classic masters. However, tectonic motifs also were given weight and emphasis only by degrees: the symmetry in the painting of the Sistine Madonna cannot be found earlier, and the vertical speaks so strongly that we are tempted to believe that it was first discovered here. If, in fifteenth-century paintings, the skeleton of the rule is frequently given even greater prominence, it is nonetheless only the skeleton. The essential difference between the primitives and the classic artists is that, in the works of the latter, form and content coincide, and no external schema is superimposed on the picture. When Perugino, in his fresco, "The Delivery of the Keys to St. Peter," divides the group into two perfectly even halves, the regularity of the order has a very striking effect; yet the symmetry in Raphael's "Death of Ananias" is not only richer but more rigorous and, above all, has more objective justification than that of the earlier painting. In the Raphael, the raised central dais on which the apostles stand represents authority; and the coming and going of the people are parallel, but naturally separate, events. In Perugino's painting, there exists no cogent reason for the division of the group of disciples. Conversely, Raphael knew very well what he was doing when he avoided a symmetrical arrangement in the tapestry of "St. Paul in Athens," a scene closely related to "The Delivery of the Keys to St. Peter."

The foregoing also provides the answer to the other question that relates to the role assigned to the tectonic in great Italian art. Tectonic composition was used only when it resulted naturally from the subject itself. But it is true that architectonic situations are much more in keeping with the Italian outlook than with the German. Only the Italians understand architecture as a reflection of individuality; they therefore require that their painting have an architectonic basis and architectonic treatment of the figure in a degree that carries it far from the German sensibility.

Architectonic order retained this role even when the strict interpretation subsequently made way for a looser one. That Northern Italy always had a less rigorous attitude toward formal regularity is not of great concern to us here; however, Titian and even Correggio were, in their outlook, more fundamentally architectonic than any German artist. The relaxation of rule on such a basis has, of course, an entirely different meaning from the fundamentally loose order of the North.

2. By examining and comparing a number of pictorial themes, we shall easily find suitable opportunity to clarify this fundamental attitude in some of its further manifestations.

Leonardo, in his "Last Supper" (Fig. 36), gave the first great model of the classic treatment of a narrative subject according to strict tectonic laws. Christ is seated at the center of the table—a single figure between equal numbers of apostles to His right and His left; the latter are divided into two groups of three on each side. The accompanying architecture is, for the first time, attuned exclusively to the figures; and the plane-like appearance of the mural is so strongly emphasized that in it, too, a tectonic note seems to be sounded. In contrast to all earlier representations, this picture produces an incomparable impression of composure. The dominating power of the central figure, as a central figure, is in itself unique. The northern spectator, too, will be struck by the revelation of the significance of architectonic principles for an animated scene. At the same time, he will have to recognize the impossibility of transferring this type of picture to the North. Even when it is granted that a religious painting has its particular exigencies, this "Last Supper" remains, in its strictness, an exclusively Italian picture. The Germans always long for a bit of freedom; for them, there must be something somewhere that does not submit to rule, and somewhere a window must be open to let in some fresh air. No one would dare claim that, in composing this picture, Leonardo was encumbered by schematic concepts—the feeling expressed is so powerful that the form must be fully accepted as personal necessity. But when detached from its national basis, the effect always degenerates into formalism.

The genuineness of this extremely strict mode of composition is not put in doubt by the fact that the Italians themselves soon relinquished it. The centrality of the pictorial structure remained (and persisted down to the great banquets of Paolo Veronese); but the symmetrical groups of three formed by the disciples, despite the artful transformation of their similarity into dissimilarity, had to yield to the need for more fluid arrangements. (See Andrea del Sarto's "Last Supper" in Florence.)

37. Andrea del Sarto, Lamentation (Florence, Pitti)

The difference between Germany and Italy, however, can be detected readily even at this point. Dürer's design of the Last Supper in the Large Passion woodcut series is manifestly inspired by Leonardo; but how little importance is given to regularity! How little value the central figure has as axis! Even the over-all view of the interior is not presented from a central vantage point. The objection can be made that there are inherent distinctions between woodcuts and murals. Nevertheless, symmetry would not have been rejected in even the tiniest Italian print. But Dürer himself dropped symmetry completely in his later and more important versions of the Last Supper.

38. Paolo Moranda, called Cavazzola, Lamentation, 1517 (Verona)

Classic Italy was clearly more inclined to interpret an event as a plastically tangible image of groups than as an action; and this, of course, favored tectonic composition. We know we are in the South when we come upon a painting of the Visitation, of the scene where Mary visits her cousin Elizabeth in the country, which is portrayed as a group of two embracing women whose embrace is most wonderfully echoed in the spanning arch of the portico in the background (Albertinelli). It does not *have* to be that way; but, in the North, this interpretation was entirely unknown. Pontormo later replaced the portico by a closed niche (fresco in the courtyard of the Annunziata), which is practically the same. Thus the Presentation in the Temple was depicted as a group standing in front of a niche; and even less important events like the Circumcision of Christ were endowed with solemnity through this motif (Signorelli).

Circumstances permitting, the figure group itself was subordinated to strict tectonic order, not only in scenes of tranquility, such as representations of the Holy Family, but also in those of great emotion, like the Lamentation. The subtly composed pyramidal arrangement in Perugino's "Lamentation" of 1495 was, to be sure, not repeated in its artificiality—evidently, the incongruity between form and content was perceived. But, in principle, tectonic rendering of the Lamentation was possible also in the classic period, as is demonstrated by the paintings of Andrea del Sarto (Fig. 47) and Titian. If the central axis plays no role in Fra Bartolommeo's extremely noble "Lamentation," the relief-like character, by way of compensation, strongly asserts itself as a tectonic bond and is reinforced by the sustained accord of parallel horizontals.

Furthermore, a single beam of the cross, or the fragment of such a beam, in the center of the picture suffices to make the tectonic tonality felt as dominant, even when the figures are freely grouped. (See Fig. 38.)

Dürer's early attempt to compose the Lamentation in triangular form may have later seemed strange to the artist himself.

In Italy, it was taken for granted that when a standing figure constituted the spiritual center of a narrative, it would coincide with the central axis of the painting and would do so, not in an approximate way, but with precision and tectonic emphasis. This was customary not only for scenes of the Flagellation, the Crucifixion, or the Ascension, but also for situations where the centrality of the chief actor was less imperative, such as the Sermon of St. John. The Germans, on the other hand, placed the preacher in profile at the edge of the picture, with the people spread out before him. It is characteristic of their tectonic requirements that the Italians cast this story, too, in architectonic form and fully exploited the power of the middle axis by placing the orator in the center of the picture. Works by Ghirlandaio and Andrea del Sarto are well-known examples. However, even paintings where the principle figure does not occupy the center can be organized according to architectonic rules, and the important accent of the middle axis will not be lost. We are reminded

39. Matthias Grünewald, Crucifixion (Colmar, Isenheim Altarpiece)

of Raphael's "Expulsion of Heliodorus" in which the composition, to the German way of thinking, borders on artificiality and approximates a scene from opera—using that phrase in the derogatory sense. The fixed center and the exact correspondence between the groups at the sides leading into and out of the picture not only appear contradictory to the character of a sudden event but also to seem to endanger the impression of life altogether. However, Germans have no right to judge on the basis of their own attitudes when a specifically Italian concern is in question. Even Raphael did not always design his compositions so symmetrically. In the "Expulsion of Heliodorus," he considered the strictest type of order to be proper to the solemnity of the scene; it is as if the divine laws, which had been transgressed, had found expression in the structure of the painting. We repeat that the classic period treated regular order with a sense of responsibility different from that of the pre-classical period, when Ghirlandaio and Pintoricchio were in the habit of alternating rather unconcernedly between free and strict order.

The North shies away from narratives cast in tectonic form. The Germans cannot catch their breath when, in an animated event, everything is in its place according to a clear plan. Their general attitude, here too, is directed toward the immeasurability of a free rhythm. The sixteenth century, however, also clearly recognized the value of regulated order and, in contrast to the primitives, put it to good use. However, even where the pursuit of the tectonic was more vigorously pressed, it always fell short of Italian rigorousness. There are different sorts of symmetry. Dürer's "Adoration of the Trinity" has a middle axis, as does Raphael's "Disputa," which has a similar subject; but the axis in Dürer's work lacks tectonic meaning. The physiognomy of German art receives its distinctive character far more from the co-existence of opposing possibilities. Pictorial structure is firmer in the works of Dürer and Grünewald than in those of fifteenth-century painters; the horizontal and the vertical prevail as the principal directions, and the presence of a feeling for rules is unmistakable. But if the strictest regularity is realized in certain works, the excitement in the unconfined breaks forth with all the more joy in others. Dürer was of course, more than any other, the man of rules; but in him, too, an urge toward the unrestrained occasionally sought satisfaction. Grünewald was, by nature, less tectonic that Dürer; and in Altdorfer's paintings we find things which surpass all that was customary. Yet, evidently, such "formlessness" became psychologically possible only on the basis of a greater awareness of "form."

Let us again discuss a few pictorial themes.

We find the most monumental interpretation of the Crucifixion in the Isenheim Altarpiece (Fig. 39). Ought we not to expect the cross to stand in the center of the picture? It could be in the center and the painting would still not be Romanizing; but it is *not* in the center. The reason for this cannot have been Grünewald's desire to avoid the split that severs the two halves of the picture into wings that open up: he did the same thing in smaller paintings of the

40. Hans Baldung, Baptism of Christ, 1519 (Frankfurt a.M.)

Crucifixion where no such obligation existed. This feature is no
mere expedient: Grünewald's basic sensibility expressly rejected
tectonic and regular structure as inadequate. But, as mentioned
above, in German art the other kind of organization also occurs and
is not confined to the work of Dürer. We find symmetry and asymmetry used side by side in the *oeuvre* of one and the same painter
(Baldung, Altdorfer).

The over-all shape of the Isenheim Altarpiece, with its raised
center—quite common in Germany—might also have been shocking
to an Italian. Grünewald did not recoil from the irregularity of the
form; only by that irregularity was the compelling rhythm of the

41. Albrecht Altdorfer, Halt on the Flight into Egypt (Woodcut)

distribution of the figures rendered possible. The picture looks intolerably lame when it is made straight, as has been occasionally done in copies. For the same reason, we must reject all reproductions of the inner flanking pictures that omit the unilateral projection which results from the raised center. (See Fig. 55.)

A second example of free northern order is Baldung's "Baptism of Christ" in Frankfurt (Fig. 40).

If we think of Italian paintings of the Baptism of around 1500, such as those by Bellini, Cima and Francia, we realize that this subject is conducive to a purely centralized composition; indeed we can

42. Lukas Cranach the Elder, Torgau Altarpiece, 1509 (Frankfurt a.M.)

scarcely imagine the story in different form. Christ, as a frontal
figure, stands at the central axis, while St. John the Baptist and the
attending angels provide analogous contents for the sides. In the
North, however, Gerard David used these same elements to compose
his well-known contemporary painting of the Baptism (Bruges),
which, to be sure, does not lack definiteness of direction but which
completely renounces a tectonic effect. In David's painting, Christ
stands only approximately in the center of the picture plane. David
was Flemish, but a German would not have done otherwise. Even
when the Baptismal group includes only the figures of Christ and the
kneeling Baptist, as was customary in Germany, tectonic organization
would still have been possible. The two halves of the painting would
need only to be stably and convincingly balanced (the Italians also
used this type occasionally). Although Baldung (Fig. 40) evidently
had such a goal in mind and also sought symmetrical correspondence
in the placing of the angels (in which he completely transcended
the loose organization of the fifteenth century), he nevertheless did
not allow his composition to settle into a rigid structure. He did not
permit a tectonic central axis to develop. God the Father and the
dove are off-center, and everything is in flux.

The tectonic principle was not completely absent, but we feel
that it was the exception (Wolf Traut, Nuremberg). If regulated
order was used only with reservations for even so sacred a theme
as the Crucifixion, it was only fitting that a regulated representation
of the Baptism should have met with deep distrust. Characteristically,
Patenir (Vienna), with all his strict observance of the integrity of picture plane and strong emphasis on geometric elements, moved the
main figure to one side.

In his "Birth of the Virgin" (Fig. 22), Altdorfer dared an extreme loosening of the tectonic structure, although the church interior, where the scene takes place, could have offered the imagination
sufficient material for a regulated order. However, even rectangularity, as a principle of pictorial order, was allowed to become effective
only to a limited degree; and a tectonic impression was undermined
from the start by the oblique view of the stage. The Italians, also, did
not require the centralized schema for representations of the Birth of
the Virgin or of St. John, less, we may assume, because of external
compositional difficulties than for internal reasons—the story does not

43. Hans Burgkmair, Madonna and Child, 1509 (Nuremberg)

require the most solemn form. Nevertheless, the bed is always placed
parallel to the picture plane, and the stage recedes in parallel spatial
strata; thus, tectonic cohesiveness, which the Germans expressly

wished to avoid, was again achieved. Even the deathbed of the Virgin was not spared the less tranquil oblique view; and when the uneven spatial recession in the interiors of the primitives calmed down into the more distinct spatial strata of the sixteenth century, non-centralized perspective was nevertheless retained. If we examine, in this connection, Joos van Cleve's large composition of the "Death of the Virgin" (Munich) or Dürers quiet and dignified representation in the "Life of Mary" of 1510, we see how far these artists had moved away from Schongauer (Fig. 78) and how closely they were still related to him. This relationship becomes immediately apparent when we compare these works to Mantegna's purely symmetrical "Death of the Virgin" in Madrid (Fig. 77).

One consequence of the decidedly off-center perspective is the intentionally accidental effect of the way the picture world is cut by the frame. Altdorfer's work again provides characteristic examples (see the woodcut of the "Rest on the Flight into Egypt," Fig. 41, and his painting of the same subject in Berlin). Compared with these examples, all similar attempts by Correggio will appear extremely tame.

When we turn to paintings of saints containing one or more figures, we finally arrive at a realm where analogies to Italian art would be most likely to appear—their iconic purpose permits a certain degree of "unnatural" order. However, the situation here is essentially no different from that in narrative paintings. Along with strict order, we always find the completely free pattern as an alternative; and examples of the former remain tectonically one step behind the Italian devotional image. For this reason, we cannot expect a secular composition like the "School of Athens," with its systematic organization and distribution of groups, to have a counterpart in German art. It is always a mistake to want to transpose this kind of picture to the North, for it must inevitably appear "arranged" to the Germans, unless the "parallelism of form," in Hodler's sense of the phrase, imbued the geometric schema with new naturalness.

When we use as an example Cranach's Torgau Altarpiece in Frankfurt (Fig. 42), where the holy company seems to be dispersed, as if caught in a sudden gust, we are fully aware of not having chosen *the* type of German religious painting. We are interested only in the fact that the freedom of an apparently wholly unregulated order was possible in Germany and was even compatible with monumental intentions. In Italy, on the other hand, similar compositions do not occur, for, even with the boldest disturbance of order, a fundamental regularity always prevails.

It is almost unnecessary to give examples of the strictly organized devotional image. This type of painting played a relatively small role in Germany, since the task was usually assigned to sculpture. Dürer would have contributed the chief work had he ever executed that many-figured "Sacra Conversazione" for which he made sketches during and after his trip to the Netherlands. In the last of these drawings, he still vacillated between a centralized and a non-centralized perspective. A little later, the young Holbein brought German classic art to its culmination in the "Darmstadt Madonna"; yet he thought it quite natural to admit an accidental element into the strict structure by disarranging the rug at a very conspicuous place in the picture. (In the "Solothurn Madonna with Saints," the architecture is still obliquely presented.)

Even in purely symmetrical compositions, the decisive factor is always the degree to which an impression of architectonic regularity is pursued and to which the center asserts itself as tectonic backbone of the painting. Only rarely do we find this conception developed to the point where a figure designating the middle seems to be held fast, as if by a magnet, to the central axis. It does happen, however, that a figure seems to avoid the middle deliberately. We are thinking of Burgkmair's Madonna of 1509 in Nuremberg (Fig. 43) which, although brimming over with Venetian motifs, decidedly aligns itself in its composition on the anti-Italianate side. It has a Venetian marble throne; but this is combined with the German poetry of the corner, of the angle near the edge. And the dot over the "i" is the rose bush that covers the edge of the marble panel, dissolving the definiteness of plastic form into painterly intangibility at the most important point.

3. Formal consonance and dissonance or—otherwise stated— the strict and the free harmony of architecture, has its exact parallel in the treatment of the forms of the *head* and *body* and of the *pictorial whole*.

We find Raphael's tapestry of the "Miraculous Draught of

44. Raphael, The Miraculous Draught of Fishes
Chiaroscuro woodcut by Ugo da Carpi

(The composition here is slightly changed,
and is simplified as regards the accessories.)

Fishes" especially harmonious in the way the whole fits into the
frame, in the way the landscape accords with the figures. There is
the mountain range at the shore that accompanies the ascending row
of figures and the caesura produced by the unobstructed horizon of
the water that coincides with the caesura in the group. The figures
are suited to one another, as if they had all developed according to
the same law of formation; and the individual parts of the figures—
for example, the hands of St. Andrew and St. Peter—fit into the given
angles and curves as if made to order, and yet quite naturally, or
are shown against a background that seems to have been prepared expressly for them as the proper foil. All these elements are of decisive
importance for the mood of the picture. They may have been felt
for a long time before being recognized and analyzed by the intellect.
Although Raphael developed these features to an extraordinary
degree, we cannot say that they were peculiar to him personally.
They belong to the essence of the entire classic art of Italy; and they

constitute a characteristic distinction to the German manner, where lines and directions frequently seem to be in opposition to one another and to the frame. We are then tempted to speak of a harshness and roughness in the meeting of forms; but we must admit that a more harmonious adjustment would endanger the impression of natural freshness. The call for the assimilation of forms surely rang out in sixteenth-century Germany, but it was only half heard. Frankly, the Germans cannot easily tolerate the perfect harmony of the Italians for long. Even in Italy, a reaction to classic art was not long in coming. However, Michelangelo's later works or the art of Tintoretto should still be evaluated differently, since they are based on strict harmony, while the basic attitude in the North was opposed to this kind of harmony from the beginning.

And what about heads? We find Italian faces more regular than German ones, in life as in art. There is, without doubt, a connection between the natural constitution of a race and its ideal of beauty in art; but we must not assume that the portraits of Raphael, Sebastiano, or Titian were imbued with harmony as a result of a mere imitation of reality. Such an assumption is belied by the many Quattrocento heads that strongly tend toward eccentricity. The inclination to see pervasive similarities in a complex of heterogeneous forms, like those of a head, surely existed in Italy at an early date; but only the classic artists seem to have really possessed the power of experiencing the correspondence of dissimilar elements on the grounds of a unity created in nature.

No one can deny the presence of this new sense of unity in portraits by the great northern masters. Yet northern heads look different; and their zest lies precisely in the incommensurability of the individual parts, in self-assertive configurations where a completely dissimilar form thrusts up with eruptive force. It seems impossible to see certain heads by Cranach and Baldung in terms of a unified pattern. To explain this as a result of the different character of the northern models is not wholly incorrect; but similar configurations also occur in architecture, where the artist was free from all obligation to achieve likeness. The German concept of unity was always compatible with an entirely different admixture of heterogeneous elements from that found in Romance nations.

It is the same with the concept of formal unity in the human

body as a whole. The beauty of a female body by Titian or Franciabigio is for us an Italian beauty because of a homogeneity which
the Germans would have never rejected in principle but which they
had no desire to see carried out in actual practice. Dürer, to be sure,
was convinced that the Italians were on the right path, because they
followed in the footsteps of nature which, to them, always proceeded
rationally and begot its forms according to uniform laws. He devoted
extensive writings to prove that even the extremes of the very tall
and slender and of the short and stocky human figure are regulated
by a common principle. More important for art were his efforts to
demonstrate the formal consistency of the individual figure. To this
he returned again and again, evidently because he saw in it something important for Germany. He believed in the *"Vergleichlich-
keit"* [1] of shapes in organic forms; and surely his Lucretia in the
painting of 1518 appeared more perfect to him than the Eve in his
1504 engraving. But even Dürer could not acknowledge that living
things can be wholly encompassed by rules.

In any case, Dürer's theories did not become universal dogma.
It is symptomatic that even paintings that are obviously the result
of a related concern—like Baldung's pair of women, one slender and
one broad, the so-called two witches (Frankfurt)—have little similarity to Italian works as regards regularity. If we were to put it to a
vote today, the decidedly irregular configurations of German art
would probably receive the majority of ballots. We can question
whether the great abdominal curves of women by painters like
Baldung, Urs Graf, or the later Cranach, can still be classified under
the concept of harmony; but it is certain that the clear harmony
of Dürer's "Lucretia" never aroused great excitement in any spectator. It is apparently in the German nature to find the harmony of
disharmony the most interesting.

---

[1] Dürer's term for "harmony" or "congruity," in the sense of the Italian *"conformità"*
or *"concordanza."* See Erwin Panofsky, *The Life and Art of Albrecht Dürer* (Princeton, 1955), p. 276. [*Tr.*]

III. THE WHOLE AND ITS PARTS

THE INDIVIDUAL PARTS of a painting, like those of a building, are expected to form an integral whole; and this is a requirement to which both Italians and Germans would have agreed in principle. But the concept of integrality is different for each. In its strictest sense, it is valid only for Italian art. Alberti uses the word *"composizione"* to denote the making of a picture from single figures, he also employs the term for the formal totality of a head or a body, a perfectly logical use according to the meaning the word had for him. The decisive factor is the extent to which a feeling exists that self-sufficient parts can join to form a unity that is complete in itself and has the quality of inevitability.

Unified formal organization and regulated order have already been discussed, and it may appear as if nothing essentially different needed to be added. However, though the chapters partially overlap (integrality presupposes regulated order), the concept of the whole and the relation of the parts to the whole still contain something new; and the word "inevitability" takes on a deeper meaning. Regularity of sequence and harmony of form can exist without resulting in an integral whole, for formal uniformity is not identical with unity. A regular tree-lined avenue is uniform, but whether the arbored walk as such is a unity, i.e., an entity complete and perfect in itself, remains another question.

This self-sufficient perfection was precisely the aim of Italian art. It was perceived in the works of Antiquity, and Alberti's definition of beauty (inspired by Vitruvius) is entirely in the Antique spirit. He defines beauty as a formal unity in which not even the smallest part may be changed, added, or omitted without detriment to the whole.[1] Only an Italian could have said this in the fifteenth

---

[1] L. B. Alberti, *de re aedificatoria* lib. VI (at the beginning). ". . . ut sit pulchritudo quidem certa cum ratione concinnitas universarum partium in eo cujus sint: ita ut addi aut diminui aut immutari possit nihil quin improbabilius reddat."

century. However, Alberti's idea was merely a premonition that was not realized until the classic period.

This quality of unalterability acquires value only when the content is rich. The sphere and the cube are, after all, also totalities that conform to Alberti's definition; but only the Sistine Madonna or Bramante's St. Peter's provide that classic formal whole that we experience as inevitable, and that possesses, at the same time, a life transcending all reality by virtue of its fusion of extremely diverse elements into a unity. The motifs of symmetry and stressed central axis are only elementary features in the formal effect of the Sistine Madonna; the essential element is the unification of contrasting parts so that each appears to be a necessary member within an "organic" whole. It is the same with architecture. Compared with his predecessors, Bramante was a classic artist, because he introduced greater variety into the complex of forms and still achieved a unity in the whole that banishes any thought that something could be different from what it is. The spectator can then delight in the individual forms, which are complete in themselves, and at the same time feel a more sublime joy in the union of all the parts into a wonderful collective existence. Planes, solids, and volumes of various types make up a unity that should not be judged a mere treat for the eye; instead, it offers the possibility of experiencing a supernaturally enhanced existence. Had Bramante's plan for St. Peter's been fully realized, there would be no greater example of such ideality. However, in order to characterize the spirit in which this art was conceived, we have to quote Leonardo: At the contemplation of the perfect proportionality of great beauty, the soul becomes conscious of its own divine essence.

In natural science, the development from lower to higher forms of life is designated by the terms differentiation and integration. This means that the members of an organism gradually become distinct from one another while becoming, at the same time, more integral components of the whole, i.e., they become parts of such a kind that not one could be omitted without mutilation of the whole. This is precisely the meaning of development in art as well. The higher forms of organization, however, are also characterized by higher levels of vitality and vigor. The fine arts fulfill their greatest task when, arising from a natural basis, they elevate man to experiences of form in which the narrowness of his existence is forgotten. All "form" is life-enhancing.[1]

During his trip to Rome, Goethe repeatedly referred to the wonder of form; and some of his utterances lay bare the core of the matter. At the sight of the ancient temple of Assisi, he exclaimed, "How *complete!*" (In the printed version, the word was replaced by the paler "perfect.") His admiring amazement at the structure of certain organisms which he observed on the shore near Venice culminates in the sentence, "What a precious, magnificent thing is a living being! How perfectly suited to its mode of existence, how true, how *alive!*" The similarity of his reaction toward a natural creature and an artistic creation is noteworthy; art is a second nature and creates its forms according to the same principles. These concepts, however, were already familiar to the Italians from the beginning of the Renaissance.

How complete! How alive! The intensity of existence is an attribute often praised in the Italian nature and the Italian people; but, here, "existence" also possesses its special quality. The southern Renaissance conveys to us an impression of freedom and emancipation that we feel to be wholly new. Everything is articulated and moves with loose joints, as it were. The columns of a church nave or a portico, no matter how they are designed, function as independent entities that are distinct from the wall and have a life of their own. The stories of a palace, like the wings of a villa, are fashioned to give an impression of independence. This impression depends on definite proportions but, at bottom, it also presupposes a particular ease with which form has been realized in matter. It is this which makes a campanile appear light when the crowning belfry rests as an independent and articulated part on the tower, with which it nevertheless retains an organic connection. Freedom of individual existence and strictness of the total composition go hand in hand,

---

[1] The fatal double meaning of the word "form" must be discussed at this point. In artist's usage, "form" primarily means nothing more than the given object. Hildebrand, for example, used it in this sense in the (frequently misinterpreted) book title, "Das Problem der Form," by which is meant the problem that nature poses for the artist. The layman is less familiar with this use than with the other meaning, where "form" is synonymous with aesthetic pattern, configuration, or composition, as we have used it above. This is not to speak of the many other applications of the word.

here too; and the independence of the part acquires value only through its being perceived as a member of an organism that also represents a complete entity, perfect in itself.

Herein lies the great contrast to the North. Form, in Germany, must force its way through another kind of material; and, too, the will to form is different from the start. The Germans find it difficult to believe in perfection in this world. It is true that during the sixteenth century the idea of integrality and of a rigorously self-sufficient formal system was conceived in the North as well; but this was not a natural idea for the Germans. The concept of the relation of the parts to the whole adhered tenaciously to a different principle, and was as difficult to transform as the concept of the relationship of the individual to the world. This is one of the reasons for the residue of vagueness, heaviness, and cohesiveness in German architecture as compared with the Italian. However, these qualities stem not from an imperfectly developed taste but from a different physical and metaphysical attitude.

And how could this different northern feeling about life have been suppressed in the conception of the picture and the figure? Can we imagine a German contemporary of Alberti calling a body or a head a *"composizione"*? Can we believe that the manifest necessity in the union of freely existing parts, as developed by the Italians, could ever have become a generally accepted formula for seeing nature and rendering it in pictures?

For Dürer, yes. He tried to approach the world from this viewpoint, conceiving a type of beauty akin to Italian beauty. But, as soon as we try to apply the concepts of integrality and articulation to his work, we realize how deeply even Dürer's attitude was rooted in the northern inclination toward fused unseparated form. And is it not this very quality that kept his popularity alive, while Holbein, with his purer form, seems more distant to the Germans?

However, the significance of all of this lies in the fact that the values in question are supra-national possessions, in which the North could share without imitating foreign models. If the Germans arrive at syntheses different from those of the Italians, it does not mean that they are unable to understand Italian form. It may even happen that, just through their awareness of the contrast, the Germans can be more appreciative of the free articulation and strict self-containment of Italian art. The words Goethe wrote home at the beginning of his journey in Italy should be understood in this light. Goethe wrote, "The soul expands; man feels himself to be somehow transfigured and has a sense of a freer life, a loftier existence, of ease and grace." (Not included in the printed version.)

The importation of Italian products to the North would not satisfy the desires of the Germans. For them, perfection has to have arisen out of the soil of imperfection; and they are capable of enjoying this beauty only as beauty in a state of becoming and not of fulfillment.

Architecture

The Italian development in the realm of the tectonic is extremely clear with regard to our present topic.

The simplest example of the uniting of dissimilar elements into a whole is to be found where a wide central panel is combined with two narrower side panels in such a way that the triad *must* be perceived as a unity: the predominance of one part causes the others to appear as accompanying forms. This motif occurs in altars and tombs and, as the so-called "rhythmic travée" (Geymüller), was used in the pilaster order of the Cancelleria. Here, we can already speak of classic form because of the independent character of the proportions of the individual planes. While these planes are convincing in their coherence, each one has value in itself. The particular system of proportions need not concern us here; it is enough that an effect of unity is achieved compared with which the solutions of the fifteenth century easily appear disjointed.

In the Antique triumphal arches, the Italians had great models for an organism composed of diverse plane proportions. Because of the attic, the horizontal proportions have to be taken into account along with the vertical proportions; and the semicircle of the arch is allied to the rectangular form as the important contrast. Alberti early recognized and used the beauty of this combination; and later generations did not tire of approaching the mystery through increasingly precise understanding of the geometric relationships. However, even in inaccurate renderings of these monuments, which appear in exact frontal view in the backgrounds of great narrative paintings (Botticelli, Ghirlandaio, Perugino), there is always an acknowledgment of articulated unity.

The motif underwent an important modification in the prelates' tombs by Andrea Sansovino in Santa Maria del Popolo in Rome (Fig. 45). The tomb is still not completely in the grand style; but it nevertheless reflects Bramante's art and is of the greatest consequence for the development of the Quattrocento Florentine tomb into the classic Roman type. All parts are distinct and independent and are brought into a total system of free elements. The structure, interspersed with points of articulation, has, as a whole, a tighter coherency than any earlier example. Analogous forms—the side niches that repeat the shape of the main niche—are combined with decidedly contrasting ones. The main motif is the meeting of the horizontal of the reclining figure of the deceased with the verticals of the accompanying allegorical figures.

When we consider how long it was before this seemingly obvious "triumphal arch" motif took root in Germany and how completely strange and incomprehensible such a monument would have looked in a northern church of the time of Dürer, we have to admit that the explanation does not lie in the accidental absence of an ancient model, but in the existence of a fundamentally different attitude.[1]

Germany, too, had its Cinquecento; but the unitary synthesis assumed different form. It is not the unity of an arrangement of free parts, but a fluid unity in which single forms remain more or less dependent. The northern analogy to the tripartite Italian system may be found in the structure of the tripartite retable where a raised central arch is combined with two segmental side arches curving up to it. This, too, is a unity, but certainly not a unity of free elements. One example is the retable of the high altar at Breisach (Fig. 84), a characteristic transitional form of which is the Talheim Altarpiece (Fig. 13).

The same principle holds true even more strikingly in three-dimensional bodies. The central structure of the Consolazione in Todi (Fig. 35) is nearly contemporary to Sansovino's tombs. In both,

---

[1]An interesting transformation of the motif was made by Altdorfer in a woodcut (B.50) of an altar design with a manifestly Italian source.

45. Andrea Sansovino, Tomb of a Cardinal, 1507. Rome, Santa Maria del Popolo

the whole is articulated so that each part can be separated from the others or, to express it differently, so that the existence of each part is perceived as an entity. This is combined with an integrality of the whole, an absolute organic unity that depends as much on analogies of form as on contrasts. Homogeneity—the way the apses build up to the central cupola—remains an essential; but the structure acquires its real character only through the development of definite contrasts—the main rectangular body of the church has the effect of the polar opposite to the rounded forms next to it.

A northern church like the "Schöne Maria" in Regensburg

(Fig. 34) is less homogeneous (as has been mentioned earlier) and has less decided contrasts; but, above all, we feel a different vital connection of the parts. Although they are self-willed in their form, they possess no real independence. And just as the members remain confined, so the whole structure makes no claim to the completeness of a "totality." Again, this is not an entelechy. In this church, no being that carries its goal (telos) in itself has acquired form. The whole building is a complex of forms that has meaning for the Germans in terms of tension and movement; and it is not at all intended to be the image of an existence in a state of fulfillment.

Integrality and articulation—it is these that appear to the Germans as unfamiliar blessings in the Italian Renaissance. They perceive them, yet cannot adopt them as their own, because these values are in contradiction to their attitude toward life. An Italian cupola, no matter to which period it belongs, always presents the tranquil image of a clearly mounted cylinder with a culminating dome. Such cupolas migrated to Germany, too. But where the Germans were attuned to their own concept of form, they altered the cupola not only in its functional aspects, but also in its articulation. The parts are merged; and the cupola of the Frauenkirche in Dresden—where the drum no longer rests on its base like a removable part but grows out of the body of the church, so that a division is nowhere possible—has become the most highly regarded German cupola. The Dresden cupola belongs to the Baroque period; but this stylistic characterization only half describes it true character.

We call to mind the contrast between the town halls of Padua and Freiburg im Breisgau (Figs. 5 and 6), to which we referred in the first chapter. We were then concerned with the form of the single parts; now we are dealing with the relation of the parts to the whole. The impression of free articulation is based mainly on the division into stories. In Italy, even though the massive character of the wall is more strongly emphasized, there is always the feeling of matter having been conquered and penetrated by form. The northerners, on the contrary, are not at all desirous of articulation; they are carried away by the idea of a formal impetus inherent in matter, an impetus of a vaguer kind, which never arrives at the formation of distinct members. No articulations are formed in the whole or in the parts. But when the round shafts of the piers carrying the arches

46. Town Hall at Altenburg

in the Freiburg portico blend into the wall without interruption, the vagueness does not make the Germans unhappy. For them, just this state of fusion contained happiness and beauty; and the completely free Italian columned architecture lay altogether outside the sphere

47. Venice, Palazzo Manin

of the desirable or even the conceivable. It is the same with the corner
oriels, which, needless to say, have no self-contained existence; but
most characteristic of all is the fact that the building tolerates these
parasites. They seem to suck at the structure without merging with
it organically. When we consider the way the movement overlaps
onto the roof, so that even without the oriels the façade could never
be a self-contained entity, we are again made aware of the impossibility of transferring the Italian concept of the whole to the North.

    We shall supplement this comparison with some additional
examples.

    The Town Hall of Altenburg (1562-64) is classified as true
"Renaissance" (Fig. 46), but it is essentially still far removed from
the Italian concept. The stronger contrast of horizontal and vertical
motifs is new. But, even though the windows are organized into rows,
the body of the building remains unarticulated; and only the tower
and oriel have cornices that function as articulations. The oriel still

hangs on the main structure like a beehive; and a German can easily find pleasure in the way the staircase tower penetrates into the mass of the building, contradictory to all principles of Italian architecture. As a result, the whole looks more like an aggregate than a unified organism, an effect to which the gable structure on the roof contributes its full share.

The subsequent use of cornices in the Town Hall of Rothenburg (Fig. 33) was surely a declaration in favor of organic articulation; but it was a long time before such forms became really effective as articulating elements. For the present, no one would think of considering such a façade a *"composizione,"* a union of separate independent stories.

In Italy, on the contrary, articulation was so strongly felt as a fundamental principle of the Renaissance that it became indispensable even in Venice, where we would expect it least. The Palazzo Manin by Jacopo Sansovino (Fig. 47) is an example of the systematization of the Venetian palace type with its grouped middle windows, its closed side compartments, and its portico running through the entire ground story. Although the organization may have appeared somewhat too loose to the more severe Central Italian critic, from the German point of view it most decidedly has the effect of a totality composed of independent parts.

The impression of lightness and self-sufficient perfection, which depends primarily on these elements, is a property of the entire Italian Renaissance; there are, of course, gradations according to the purpose of the building. Even Baroque architecture, in spite of its tendency toward massivity, still appears more thoroughly "formed" than northern structures. The Germans willingly retained a residue of heaviness and amorphousness, even to express a wholly free and relaxed existence, as in the Old Lusthaus in Stuttgart with its round corner towers. This refers to the details of organization as well as the over-all grouping of masses. The effect of a complete existence that we admire in the Villa Farnesina and in Bramante's St. Peter's was not even sought for in sixteenth-century Germany.

The well-known portal of the Petershof in Halberstadt (Fig. 48) clearly demonstrates the requirements of the German concept of form with regard to the single parts. Since it is of a late date—1552— we have all the more reason to expect greater agreement with the

48.   Portal of the
Halberstadt   "Petershof" (1552)

foreign principles. However, the southern forms (pilasters, cornices, segmental pediments, etc.) have been completely recast within a northern matrix, so that the imports themselves have little material significance. In place of analysis, we point to a contrasting example, Giovanni della Robbia's sacristy fountain (Fig. 49), which also employs the motif of an arch framed by pilasters with a segmental pediment. Although it was made fifty years earlier and differs in function, the fountain gives a fully adequate impression of the typical contrast. In Halberstadt, the interconnectedness of an over-all movement stands out as the essential characteristic, although it does not

49.
Giovanni della
Robbia (1497)

Florence
Santa
Maria Novella

exclude the formation of independent single forms. In the Florentine work, we find the calm unity of separable parts, each of which has a life of its own, although all are necessary to the whole. The most interesting features in the Halberstadt example are the superimposed layers of curved and straight moldings above the door, which are carved in the wall and are juxtaposed to "Italian" elements placed in front of the wall. We are all familiar with these "Gothic" ribs and grooves in the jambs of doors and windows, which persisted in popular construction until the eighteenth century. They are manifestations of an urge to form that dimly fashions in stone the confined, incomplete forms seen again and again in German art. The Italian imagination of the Renaissance, in contrast, valued only fully crystallized forms.

The Italian column is, *par excellence,* such a fully crystallized form. It has importance in itself and, in that connection, was already mentioned in the first chapter. But the column reveals its true meaning as a piece of differentiated, marvelously transformed wall only in conjunction with the wall itself. Whether the series of columns

50. Florence, Interior of Sto. Spirito

belongs to a portico or is inside a church makes no difference—the forms are united in such a way that they suggest an open wall composed of these round shafts with their capitals and bases, these completely emancipated, self-contained entities, which become what they are, however, only by contrast to the solid wall. Why did German architecture neglect such effects to the point where the Germans see a peculiarly strange beauty in a Florentine arcaded basilica like Sto. Spirito (Fig. 50)? These effects are not entirely absent from the North; but form that is so strongly differentiated and self-sufficient was regarded there with mistrust. Quite apart from differences in proportions, the German supports are incorporated in the total structure in a vaguer way. Besides the column, Italy, too, used the pier, which is less distinctly separated from the wall; but even then the forms are free and complete. The piers of the Marienkirche in Halle (Fig. 73) are of an entirely different kind: they are less differentiated from the vaulting and receive their character from a peculiar state of suspension between dependent and independent existence. Therein lies a great fascination. And where the column was adopted by German architects, it will appear most vital to the Germans precisely when it does not seem to be governed wholly by its own laws.

Are we to say that, in the North, the impulse toward complete self-reliant form is unable to work its way out of matter and thus remains partially unfulfilled? This conclusion would be incorrect, since that goal does not even exist for the Germans. On the contrary, they see a positive good in the vaguer connections of form, in the struggling and developing rather than the mature and complete. With this feeling as a background, the perfect beauty of Italian art may momentarily appear to the Germans as a liberation; but they always desire to return to the dimmer spheres of the unfulfilled.

The Pictorial Image

In the same way, classic Italian art understood the composition of a picture as a totality in which contrasting parts function like members of an organism and still seem to possess complete independence within the whole. As a result, the picture has an effect of freedom and, by the inevitability of the coherence of its parts, produces the impression of an enhanced life.

We have already mentioned Raphael's Sistine Madonna as the best-known example of the classic conception of the whole. The qualities that give this painting its formal uniqueness in relation to all preceding works are those designated by the concepts of differentiation and integration. We find cultivation of contrasts along with the most rigorous unity, absolute compactness with full freedom for the individual figure. Such groups of three appear in earlier paintings; but in these, the arrangement is always somewhat loose. The components are more similar to one another; and if they seem free, this freedom merely means that they have not been integrated into the whole. Raphael's painting is a totality where the parts mutually affect one another—in other words, an organism. This organism is rich in contrasts that are not arbitrary variations but are felt as complementary. Each part supports the other: The erect main figure and the kneeling side figures; the elevation of the Madonna and the

51.
Titian
The Murder of
St. Peter Martyr

After an
engraving by
F. Zuliani

sinking of the Pope and St. Barbara; the upward glance of the Pope
and the downward-looking St. Barbara; the outward pointing gesture
of one and the inward-reaching of the other. We are reminded of the
two sides of a balance, in connection with which it is self-evident that
the contrasts that make up the pictorial system are simple and occur
only once.

Whether the order is tectonic or not has no importance for the
effect: Titian's powerful picture of the "Martyrdom of St. Peter
Martyr" (Fig. 51) produces the same impression without having a
central axis. We feel the unity of contrasting and fully independent
forms. The decisive factor is not mere consonance, found, for example, in the correspondence between the direction of the figure of the
fleeing man and the diagonal tree trunk and in the setting of this

52.
Burgkmair
St. John
at Patmos
1518

Munich
Pinakothek
(Frame
is modern)

figure against a matching atmospheric background. Only the absolute completeness of the opposition of simple contrasts gives the composition its classic character; and thus, in accordance with Alberti's words, nothing can be changed, added, or taken away without destroying the whole.

No analysis will ever be able to explain fully how this ultimate perfection is achieved. For our purposes, it is sufficient to establish that this unity is present, and that it is combined, here too, with a thorough articulation of the picture that guarantees the specifically Italian appearance of ease.

A comparison with Burgkmair's "St. John at Patmos" of 1518 (Fig. 52), which is related to Titian's picture in several respects, well illustrates the enduring difference, even though the two works

53. Sixt von Staufen, Locherer Altarpiece, 1522-24 (Freiburg im Breisgau, Cathedral)

are of different dates. In Burgkmair's painting, a figure is also co-ordinated with the movement of diagonal tree trunks; and both pictures have an enclosing vertical at the right. However, Burgk-mair's panel is not entirely self-contained but spreads out into the wings (not illustrated here) with its trees. Furthermore, it is neither articulated throughout nor composed in complementary contrasts. Rather, it is as if one part runs into the other. To understand this clearly, we have only to realize the structural significance, in the Titian, of the diagonal figure's carefully suited atmospheric back-ground, and to see how little Burgkmair aimed at making the figure

54. Hans Baldung, Lamentation. Drawing, 1513 (Basel)

of St. John really independent and at placing him against a self-contained background area.

Nevertheless, the northern Renaissance also had a new concept of pictorial unity. Although the same results were not achieved, the sixteenth century, here too, saw the horizontal and vertical directions developed with new appreciation for their stabilizing value. In one way or other, they are perceptible in all compositions. In the Talheim Altarpiece (Fig. 13), the main motif remains, of course, a configuration of three upright forms; but the musical angels introduce a connecting horizontal that acts as preparation for the embracing canopy. Even so tame a work as the "Madonna Misericordia" of the Locherer Altar in Freiburg im Breisgau (Fig. 53) contains a stronger contrast between the cloak and the standing figure than that in earlier works, since it belongs to the sixteenth century. And in the Gemmingen Tomb (Fig. 32), the pronounced horizontal of the empty middle area intersects the vertical form of the whole, which thereby gains not only greater tranquility but, above all, tighter coherence. And what are we to say of the great painted creations of the new style? In the Isenheim "Crucifixion" (Fig. 39), the powerful horizontal movement that counters the vertical of the hanging figure of Christ is entirely new. Such contrasts can be interpreted as the expression of a heightened need for vigor; but, without doubt, they also have a function in terms of a new pictorial unity. This Crucifixion is as grandly conceived as any of the classic Italian compositions, but it manifests a different concept of unity. As important as the figures are as individual entities, the predominant impression is still determined by the sweep of over-all movement. Even uniformity in the sizes of the figures was sacrificed to the great rhythmical motif without any sense of unnaturalness. Three different scales were used; and, strangely enough, we are not even aware of it at first.

Dürer was more apt to use conventional patterns that undeniably sometimes held his imagination in check. We are thinking of his paintings, for he worked with greater freedom in his graphic production. The importance of the ideal of "composition" in the Italian sense grew in proportion to the increase in the plasticity of the single forms. To a certain degree, it is possible to combine a plastic conception of the figure with the oneness of "painterly" flux; but, basically, this involves a contradiction. The most characteristic expressions of

55. Matthias Grünewald, Resurrection (Colmar, Isenheim Altarpiece)

the German pictorial concept are those works in which the artist preserved his naïveté with regard to plastic demands, i.e., those works where plastic rendering of the figure goes no further than is required by the idea of over-all movement.

Baldung Grien's drawing of the Lamentation (Fig. 54)—for his painting of 1513 in Innsbruck—serves to illustrate the point. This is

a work we might have used as an example in the first chapter, where
the emphasis was on the single figure; our present discussion, however, is focused on the picture as a whole. The drawing displays maňy
sixteenth-century innovations that parallel Italian tendencies: the
development of the body of the dead Christ as a guiding, filling form
that is decisive for the picture as a whole; the emphasis on contrasts
of direction; and the correspondence between the verticals of the
cross, the figures, and the side edges of the picture. However, given
a traditional conception that demanded so little plasticity from the
figures, an entirely different type of composition and pictorial unity
was bound to result. The body of Christ is distinct, but it is almost
impossible to clarify the dense thicket of forms surrounding Him;
and it is just this that makes the main motif stand out so strongly.
But a unity that can be understood as a system of independent parts
has not been achieved—the whole remains a swelling sea of forms
from which a wave rises at one spot to a climactic crest of maximum
power and visibility.

We need not consider those Italian paintings where architectonic structure already paves the way for articulation. Italy, too,
produced free compositions, and these do not always have the high
degree of unity of works by Titian or Raphael. But even a loose
structure like that of Cavazzola's "Lamentation" (Fig. 38) is still a
composition of distinct parts and strives to give the impression of a
complete whole; and this impression is not impaired by the cutting
of the cross by the frame. In contrast, Baldung's drawing still contains, along with integrating elements, essential motifs that are intended to lead the spectator beyond the limits of the picture.

This northern problem of dependent-independent existence has
particular significance for the winged altarpiece. Here, several pictures are joined to produce a total effect. This in itself need not exclude full development of the single picture; but, in German art, the
very dependence of each part had to be stressed as well.

The paintings of the Annunciation and Resurrection (Fig. 55)
on the wings of the Isenheim Altarpiece are just such dependent-
independent creations. We *can* grasp each one singly; but, all the
same, we feel that they both gravitate inwards, i.e., refer to a center
lying outside their frames. There is sublime grandeur in the way the
steep diagonal from left to right in the "Annunciation" is followed

56.
Leinberger

High Altar
at Moosburg
(1513)

by an ascent that leads in a single sweep through the double scene in
the central panel up to the intense light in the "Resurrection." Thus,
the (relative) dependence of the center painting is left in no doubt.

The customary procedure, followed in Martin Schaffner's Wetten-hausen Altarpiece (Munich, Pinakothek), was the symmetrical co-ordination of four panels; but, as always, this was done in such a way that the outer pictures—here, the "Annunciation" and the "Death of the Virgin"—are clearly stamped as outer paintings through their spatial perspective. Furthermore, the two pictures refer to each other in the complementary diagonals of the descending dove on one side, and the ascending soul on the other.

The wings of Lukas Cranach's Torgau Altarpiece (Fig. 42) had already been designed in the same manner. In spite of their indi-vidual importance, their great diagonals clearly indicate their need of each other's support; even the central panel is complete only together with the wings. Although more definite differentiation of the single panels according to their position in the altarpiece ap-peared only in the sixteenth century, a tradition of unification had already existed early in the fifteenth. It was not present to the same extent in all regions of Germany; but it was precisely in Franconia that artists thought at an early date in terms of unified composition, as is shown, for example, by the Munich Pinakothek's Hof Altarpiece. Here, the parts are no longer interchangeable, and the individual panel becomes alive only within the total context. Surprising results have already been achieved by restoration of original ensembles, but much is still to be done. Above all, we must take this fact into account in relation to the aesthetic inadequacy of many pieces that, originally included, in a larger whole, now hang in museums as single paintings and thus have a certain quality of lameness.

Hence, a process of formal unification took place in the North as well as in the South; but the concepts of unity were different. Al-though Germany also manifested an inclination toward articulated systematization, the predominant tendency was in the direction of an over-all flowing movement in which neither the individual part nor the whole were allowed to terminate decisively.

The fifteenth-century tradition exemplified in the lofty tripartite structure of Riemenschneider's "Altarpiece of the Holy Blood" in Rothenburg was continued in the direction of greater cohesiveness in the Moosburg Altarpiece by Hans Leinberger (Fig. 56). Dürer would have surely rejected the motif in this form; but this does not mean that such a magnificent upward-flowing *élan* is to be considered

57.
Jacopo Sansovino
Bacchus   Florence

an epilogue to an outmoded art: here, as always, the duality of the
German concept of form asserts itself. Thus, even the Gemmingen
Tomb (Fig. 32)—where the vertical is intersected by a complementary horizontal—is related to the Moosburg Altarpiece and is a
stranger to all Italian art. In neither work are the parts absolutely independent; and even Backofen did not aim at an impression of compactness, the rounded arch notwithstanding. The flame does not lick
as high as in Leinberger's altarpiece, but the forms still lose themselves in indefiniteness.

    This attribute remained characteristic of German art even when
Gothic forms had been completely replaced by Renaissance motifs.
We see evidence of this in the later memorial plaques and altarpieces,

whose piled-up forms are so fundamentally opposed to the Italian concept of integrality.

The Head and Body

It seems natural for the body to be conceived as an articulated whole; and we may believe that people everywhere felt the same in this respect, although manifold possibilities for welding the parts into a unity are imaginable. However, this is not the case. The feeling for the body as a whole and for the function of the limbs within the whole exists in very different degrees. These variations have great historical significance, since the physical bearing reflects the metaphysical attitude in the most direct way.

Corresponding to the articulating Italian concept of the body is an unhampered mobility of the joints. This mobility is always linked with a strong interest in anatomical structure; but, in the last analysis, it corresponds to a particular attitude toward life. We can disregard all else that determines the character of a figure like Sansovino's "Bacchus" (Fig. 57): the free action of the limbs within a body perceived as a totality is in itself characteristic of Italian art. But when we ask why such a figure was not possible in Germany, we at once encounter fundamental contrasts in the attitude to life, contrasts that retain their importance when we carry the comparison into other spheres of thought and feeling. Italian art, free and articulated, remains akin to the art of Antiquity; the northern man, however, conceived the body in a vaguer context and saw truth more in a flowing current of forms than in a divisive formal structure.

To illustrate this tendency, we must turn less to Dürer than to "the others." Much in Dürer's drawing of nudes of 1504 (Fig. 27) was taken over from Italian-Antique patterns. We note the differentiation of the torso from the lower limbs, the articulation of the chest and abdomen, and the cultivation of contrasts of form and direction. All these features indicate an interpretation altogether different not only from that in Riemenschneider's "Adam" (Figs. 30 and 31) and particularly Schongauer's "St. Sebastian" (Fig. 18), but also from Cranach's in his "Adam" of 1528 (Fig. 20). The latter are all related and represent, either in the earlier or in the more freely developed

58. Franciabigio, Venus (Rome)   59. Baldung, Allegory, 1529 (Munich)

style, an intermediate line in German art, which Dürer had the cour-
age to renounce. The focus in these pictures is not on articulation
and strong contrasts, but rather on fusion and the unified flow of
forms. The drawing of the torso does not seek to dissect the form into
autonomous parts and to bring out directions counter to the dominant vertical; instead, it keeps within the general direction of the
movement and suppresses rather than emphasizes the separating
boundaries. It is remarkable that even the natural articulation tends
to disappear and that the limbs are more tightly bound, as it were,
to the body. Even more striking is that, in contrast to Dürer's

"Adam," the whole figure is somewhat—we do not want to say un-
stable—but still somewhat unfulfilled and is not complete in itself.
These qualities illustrate well the German concept of integrality and
are also applicable to the evaluation of German architecture.

For a confrontation of original Italian form with a German
example, the comparison of Franciabigio's "Venus" (Fig. 58) with Baldung's "Allegorical Figure with a Mirror" (Fig. 59) suggests itself,
since both have similar motifs: one arm raised, the head turned, and
the other arm hanging down. This similarity, however, is completely
canceled out by the dissimilarity in the conception of form. The
uninterrupted current of movement is again—and here even more
strongly—characteristic of the forms of the German painter. The
Italian, on the other hand, sought a harmony of clearly separated
parts as well as the excitement of contrasting directions. Of course
these are extremely precise proportions that have been harmonized
to produce an over-all system of relationships. In Baldung's painting,
we completely forget the question of the parts and their proportions
because of the powerful total torrent of forms. A certain vagueness
about the joints creates the impression that the limbs are less flexible;
and, as far as the whole is concerned, the difference is that the Italian
figure is completely self-contained, while the other cannot be detached from the background without suffering some loss of stability.
We have discussed this earlier. It is undeniable that the sixteenth-century Germans, and Baldung in particular, were also aware of other
possibilities; but the tangled interplay of forms remained the rule
and statuesque isolation, the exception.

The distinction between the two peoples stands out as clearly
in the design of the head as in the conception of the body, although
the leeway for variation in the interpretation of the forms seems even
more limited. In German art, the portrait head was of course a much
more important theme than the nude. We might even say that if
nothing but a few portraits had survived, they would suffice to give
a complete idea of the grand spirit of the sixteenth century. We think
first, of course, of Dürer's late monumental heads; but these do not
exhaust the phenomenon of German design. Dürer's heads have their
stylistic meaning in the uniformly clear perception of bounded form
and in the conception of the head as a severe formal system. But Baldung's or Cranach's have greater freshness. We cannot characterize

60. Raphael, Count Castiglione (Paris)

the difference by calling the latter less discriminating; here, too, the decisive contrast is the opposition between a conception of form in association with flowing movement and a more articulating divisive kind of design.

Lukas Cranach's portrait of Dr. Scheuring of 1529 (Fig. 21) is well suited for comparison with Dürer's portrait of Holzschuher

61. Hans Baldung, Portrait of an Unknown Man, 1514 (London)

(1526), even to the locks of hair falling on the forehead. We find
Cranach to be somewhat more cautious in the function-enhancing
design of single motifs like the glance and the hair; but the flow of
lines is extremely exciting. The merging of the eye sockets with the

temples and the cheekbone is a unique sight, next to which the Dürer appears almost cool. The fact that the hands are still confined enhances the effect of freedom of the upper part of the picture.

The situation in Baldung's portrait of a bearded man of 1514 (Fig. 61) is a similar one. Compared to the Dürer, the painting may have a disorderly and confined appearance, in which the relationship of the figure to the frame and the vigorously jutting forms in the costume play an important role. But what directness in the lines of this head with its melancholy glance, its arched eyebrows, and its long nose, which, by overlapping the silhouette, has become the dominant element! (A resemblance to Dürer's drawing of his mother is not to be overlooked; but, on the other hand, that drawing has no equivalent in Dürer's painted work.)

In Raphael's contemporary portrait of Count Castiglione (Fig. 60)—which is on a much larger scale—it is the tectonic system that primarily determines the effect: the way the forehead is superimposed as a horizontal form on the upright form of the face; the way the nose as a vertical is held fast within this upright, while the eyes, cheekbones, and mouth echo the horizontal of the forehead. However, the eyes, independently of their natural form, have value in themselves in the same way as the pilaster intervals in a façade: they are autonomous and, at the same time, essential in their place within the whole. Thus, the entire silhouette of the sitter is set into the rectangle of the panel as a self-sufficient form.

This mode of observation offers no insight into the art of Baldung or Cranach, although they, too, thought in terms of contrasts and a different kind of unity from that of the fifteenth century. Only in the case of Dürer can we speak of comparability—but not similarity—to the Italian conception. This comparability grew with Bruyn, Aldegrever, and Holbein; but the tradition that stamps a German head as German never died out completely.

IV. RELAXED TENSION

IN HIS DEFINITION of ancient art, Winckelmann included the quality of "serenity." Since that time, views on the essential nature of Antiquity have changed somewhat, and Winckelmann's judgment is considered one-sided. However, even today, the northerner, when confronted by colonnaded southern architecture and the low southern gable, is greatly surprised at the tranquility of these buildings, whether they be from Antiquity or from the Renaissance.

It is a curious fact, that, while the Italians are much livelier in speech and gesture than the Germans, a German city or street creates a more animated impression. Various reasons may be found for this, some of which have been mentioned in the preceding chapters. In the present chapter, we do not refer to "painterly" richness and "painterly" movement, but rather to the moving force or impetus within the form. Speaking figuratively, we do not mean the vibration of an agitated surface in general, but the energy with which the single wave surges up. German form contains more activity, more tension.

It is not that tension is absent in the South—no living form is without tension—but the tension is a slacker one. The column rises and supports effortlessly; scarcely any strain is visible in the ascending wall, and the impression of calm is completed by the tranquilly suspended modillions of the cornice. All proportions here have a different ratio of height to width; they are presented as the expression of a quietly breathing existence, even when the spirit becomes austere. It is different in the North. There, we experience the strain of exertion, while, in Italy, we feel the calm of fulfillment of a being that is not dead but whose tension is slackened.

Even where it has broken with Gothic verticality and functions within "natural" proportions, northern architecture preserves an active character, which can increase to violence and impetuousness in the whole and in every detail. The very same properties distinguish German drawing from the Italian. The specific character of German figures comes from the fact that all forms are experienced in terms of tension. However, the formative power also asserts itself with a particular energy in every plant and every leaf. A determined will seems to have swelled the clouds and forced up the mountains.

This inner movement should not be confused with external movement. Michelangelo's figural motifs are, of course, more powerful than those of Dürer, and his contraposto has no equal in Germany. Yet we have to admit that even the mighty "Day" from the Medici tombs is relatively calm next to Dürer's very rigid St. Paul in his painting of "The Four Apostles"; the latter stands absolutely motionless, but the energy of his glance and the impulsive force of his drapery are stupendous.

In general, there is no difference between Grünewald and Dürer: when Grünewald, as a draftsman, models an arm by following its roundness with long drawn-out, serried parallel curves, it is also an occurrence of activated form. That Grünewald and Dürer possess this dynamic quality to different degrees is of no significance here, nor is Grünewald's more intense characterization of materials. The contrast to the Italian style of drawing remains the same in each. However, one qualification needs to be made: these traits are specific to South German art. North Germany lacks these extreme tensions, a fact that holds good in architecture as well.

Regional differences existed in Italy, too; and the full beauty of the tranquilly flowing line was not achieved until the sixteenth century. However, if anything permits us to talk of the indestructible character of the Italian concept of form, it is this line. But where are its bases to be found? We shall be inclined to seek them, first of all, in the natural feeling of the race for the body and for movement. The way a man leans against the door jamb of a house; the way a woman lifts a jug from a well—these things look different in the South than in the North. All work is handled in a different manner; and it ought to be possible to establish certain correspondences between life and general concepts of form. People in the North move more abruptly, more jerkily. Above all, their movements generally seem to depend on a determined application of will. The fruitful point of comparison lies precisely here. With all its vivacity, the Italian gesture (in the broadest sense of the word) is realized easily and effortlessly. The Germans always reckon on some resistance that has to be overcome. They interpret everything in terms of a will that wants to break through. Thus the image of the world becomes fundamentally different. At the same time, however, it becomes clear that other and deeper factors are involved than those that can be grasped through certain experiences of physical life. In the last analysis, we are confronted by the problem of the relation of form to matter and by the different interpretations of these concepts.

Pictorial Representation

We may assume that when Dürer arrived in Italy, nothing seemed stranger to him than the quality in Italian art that we call "serenity." There was neither stress nor strain in the architecture. With gentle animation, ornament spread itself over tranquil planes; similarly, in painting, line and modeling had a perfectly calm appearance. To a German, this must have been barely comprehensible and almost intolerable. And, in point of fact, we find that nothing of the real style of the much-admired Giovanni Bellini entered Dürer's work. In his youth, Dürer once copied some engravings by Mantegna, directly tracing the outlines of the figures. It is extremely characteristic that as soon as he drew freehand, he immediately made the forms more active. Dissatisfied with Mantegna's modeling by parallel hatching, he followed the volumes with strokes that tightly clasp the forms as if with hands. Dissatisfied with the design of the plants, he gave the shoots more vigor. And it is the same throughout.

These qualities are not only characteristic of Dürer; they also constitute an outstanding trait of all German drawing throughout the whole period and set it off from that of the Italians.

We turn first to two paintings discussed in the preceding chapter, the standing nudes by Franciabigio and Baldung Grien (Figs. 58 and 59). No one will deny the dissimilarily of effect with respect to calmness and turbulence of form. But the essential factor is not the different bodily structure—for example, the strikingly high abdomen in Baldung's painting; it is rather the way in which the German

makes action operative within the form. We can see this clearly in
the turn of the head, in the shoulder joint, and in the straightened
knee. However, even apparently motionless form is charged throughout with tension, so that the thighs or the hanging arm acquire an
entirely different look. Even the design of the abdomen gains its
energy less through the roundness *per se* than through the action of
projecting. How tranquil is the plasticity of the Italian body and how
comprehensible is its connection with the relaxed movement! The
same is true of the entire picture: it is the distinction between the
quietly flowing Italian ornament and the more impulsive German
tendril.

For additional illustrations, we turn to the reclining nude as
conceived by Giorgione and Titian (Fig. 62), and to their German
counterpart in a painting by Cranach (Fig. 63). The latter can hardly
have been created without such Italian models and may therefore be
all the more instructive for our comparison. The individual contrasts between Cranach and Baldung pale into insignificance next to
the pervasive national similarity in their concepts of form. Without
doubt, the long peaceful line in the Titian (and in the Giorgione)
could not have matured before the sixteenth century, for the Quattrocento was shorter-winded. But Cranach's fidgety figure nevertheless denotes a "High Renaissance" for Germany and not a mere in-
troduction. The treatment of the crossed legs with their outspread
toes is extremely characteristic. The difference in the motifs of movement should be pointed out: In one picture, the legs are stretched
out with grace and ease, while in the other they are crossed, with the
crossing taking place above the knee. But the deeper contrast lies in
the conception of form as such, so that every part of the body in the
Cranach appears to be filled with tensions different from those in the
Titian. This different kind of life is, of course, also reflected in the
picture as a whole.

If Dürer's work occasionally has a more tranquil effect than
Cranach's, it does not mean that it falls short of Cranach's in the
intensity of the specific experience of form. But Dürer exercised, at
least in his later years, visible restraint and confined the expression of
tension within strict limits. We can sense this restraint in his standing
Lucretia (1518), as well as in his late portraits. Even the Holzschuher
portrait (1526), where Dürer surrendered himself more than usual

62. Titian, Venus (Florence)

to sweeping line, remains more controlled in its formal structure than Cranach's related head of Dr. Scheuring of 1529. (See Fig. 21.) But since we are interested at present only in the confrontation with Italian examples, Cranach's style of drawing is the more instructive for us. In its bold gripping manner, this style was surely more easily comprehensible to the German public than the "academically" disciplined later Dürer.

The intertwining of form, which in itself presupposes movement, was already discussed in the first chapter. Now, more than that is intended—the intensity of movement that is inherent in every form, in the bony and in the fleshy parts, in the line of the mouth, as well as in individual tufts of hair. Everything is made clear by the comparison of Cranach with an Italian like Raphael (see Fig. 60). How expressive are the tensions in this head by Cranach; how thrilling the ups and downs! How the cheekbone juts out; how the hollows dig in! How much activity is contained in the drawing of the eyes! Certainly, there are exaggerations; but Cranach needed these exaggerations to

63. Lukas Cranach the Elder, Nymph of the Fountain, 1518 (Leipzig)

be able to do justice to his perception of form. A whole treatise could be written solely on the movement of locks of hair in German art.

In order to also allow Dürer a say in this connection, we mention one of his earlier portraits—one of 1500 of a young man usually claimed to be Dürer's brother, Hans. The bony head is characteristically northern in its structure alone; but still more is it the almost violent energy in the treatment of the form that makes any comparison with Italian heads impossible. (The style is echoed in the forms of the numerals of the inserted date.)

As for the clothed figure, everyone knows of the great pains that northern artists took with drapery folds. It is as if they could never get enough of the interplay of these creases. We have already demonstrated how essential they are as conductors of movement in a picture. We now pick up the subject once again, this time to show that, here too, the specifically northern quality depends on the different degree of tension.

Dürer takes the lead over all the others. The mantle of St. Paul in the Munich painting of the apostles and the draperies in the Heller Altarpiece—to mention only the best-known examples—are filled

64.
Dürer
Portrait of   Munich
Hans Dürer   (1500)

with a strength of activity possessed neither by Raphael, nor by Fra
Bartolommeo, nor by any other Italian painter. These folds, severe
and straight, can be combined with high moral pathos; in the North,
even the Good is understood not as the natural fruit of a beautiful
spirit but rather as something that must be wrested from the spirit
with the greatest expenditure of force. Grünewald does not share in
this ideality of drapery folds, but he is just as great and just as singular in the fury of passionately swirling garments. His Magdalene
at the Cross in the Isenheim Altarpiece comes to mind; how strange
such a figure would look in an Italian painting! The robe and mantle
of Christ that are held by angels in Baldung's painting of the Baptism (Fig. 40) may occasion further comparison. Italian drapery has
grandeur and great thematic variety; but it lacks precisely that which
constitutes the distinctive quality of Baldung's painting: the energy
in the tracks of the folds, in their breaks and swirls. Sixteenth-century Italy was even particularly concerned with transforming a certain sharpness inherited from older art into relaxation.

To a pronounced degree, the Germans understood nature, in its

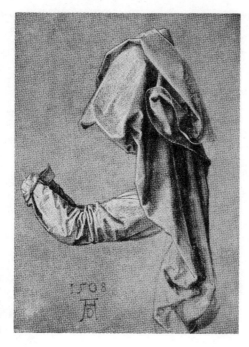

65.
Dürer
Drapery Study
for the Heller
Altarpiece

Drawing
1508 (Vienna)

entire range of creations, as an event, as an action. How passive a tree appears in southern paintings; and how little the drawing betrays of that northern will to render perceptible the upward thrust of the trunk, the spreading out of the branches, the clasping of the bark! In the work of certain northern artists, the representation of the leaves on outstretched hanging boughs is intensified almost to the impression of cascades. But even the feeling for the grain of an inanimate plank of wood completely reveals the difference between North and South. Nothing in Italy is comparable to the mysterious impulse of the lines of the grain in Schongauer's or Dürer's engravings.

Similarly, the movement of flowing and swirling waters, the undulation of the ground, and atmospheric phenomena were interpreted in a fundamentally different way.

How could the North have possibly accepted the line of relaxed tension found in Italian fountain basins, Italian tendril ornament, Italian balusters? As a matter of fact, the natural reaction was long one of resistance; and Italian form was transformed into abrupt, thrusting, straining, and compressed form. The impetus of a tendril

66. Minelli, Ornament from S. Antonio. Padua

by Schongauer (Fig. 67) is still alive in the work of Dürer, just as the relaxed movement of Italian ornament of the High Renaissance (Fig. 66) was present in Italy from the beginning on. Finally, however, this different beauty found a reverberation in the North; but we may be sure that it seemed like a sound from another world. The difference is this: that which was natural in Italy could, at first, be seen by the Germans only as something strangely refined.

Architecture

If we are to analyze in terms of single motifs the difference in the character of architecture from the viewpoint expounded above,

67.
Martin
Schongauer

Ornament
Engraving

we are surely justified in beginning with the gable. For the Germans, the feeling of being in the South is directly connected with the calm form of the low gable, whereas the steep gable can scarcely be imagined separate from the image of a northern city. This low gable of the Renaissance is, of course, a direct descendant of the Antique pediment; and the predominance of the obtuse-angled saddle-roof between the gables was never seriously threatened, even during the Gothic period. Similarly, the North could not easily give up its steep gable, since it corresponded to the traditional steep roof necessary for practical reasons. Nevertheless, here as little as elsewhere should necessity be assigned the sole responsibility for the form. Other solutions could have been, and later were, found. However, when the Jesuit church in Munich (Michaelskirche) was built in the second half of the sixteenth century (Fig. 68)—the first great ecclesiastical monument in the grand style patterned after Italian models—the architect regarded as self-evident the termination of the

68. Munich, Church of St. Michael
(The circular window is from a later period. The rows of niches formerly corresponded to each other.)

façade by a steep triangle rather than by a low gable. No one will
want to say that he thereby contradicted the formal character of the
rest of his façade, which, indeed, also deviates greatly from Italian
stylistic principles.

    The steep gable is manifestly a more active form than the low
gable. Secular architecture in the North also made frequent use of
the steep gable, and the German city has entire streets with walls
notched in this lively manner. But, as we know, every gabled house
has also an eaves side; and when this eaves side, with its horizontal

69. Rothenberg o.T., Hegereiterhaus

termination, is turned toward the square or the street, it asserts itself
with equal force next to the other type. Why is it that, even here,
there is no similarity to the Italian horizontality of the top of a building? The reason is essentially to be found in the roof, which, as a
large weighty form, plays an integrating role in the effect; and it
plays this role not only because it is large and visible, but also because
the house is completed only through its roof. There is no self-sufficient façade whose (larger or smaller) roof can be imagined removed
like a hat. On the contrary, the strength of the effect lies precisely in
the way the over-all ascending flow of energy permeates the roof as
well. This is the aesthetic function of the very expressive projecting
forms on the German "Renaissance" roof; and it has, of course, a different meaning than does the escape, in an Italian palace, of surplus
vertical energy beyond the top cornice, say into a balustrade with free-
standing figures (as in Sansovino's Library in Venice).

70. Padua, Courtyard of the University

As the solids in German architecture became plumper and more substantial (a development that can be well verified by comparison of the new building of the Rothenburg Town Hall with the medieval one, see Fig. 33), the great effects of activity were more decidedly cultivated. However, the active character should not be narrowly understood as an upward thrust. It exists in low heavy forms as well as in ascending ones; and the crowding of heterogeneous forms, one pushed into the other—staircase towers and the like—belongs here equally well. (See Fig. 69.) But the vertical movement never allows the heaviness and the resistance of the material to be forgotten.

We are brought back to statements made in the first chapter:

Italy sought the self-contained form, and the North saw action as the essential. Therefore, it was a long time before the emergence in the North of a feeling for the Italian plane and Italian space, with their blend of alertness and calm, and for those proportions of relaxed tension in which the beauty of Italian art is contained. On the wall were placed the serried rows of vertical moldings, which constitute the direct opposite to the Italian panel organization. When a system of surface divisions found a foothold in Germany, nonetheless, the surface proportions were still not the Italian ones. In the ceiling, the interest is focused on the cross beams and, in a vault, on the ribs, even though the latter no longer function as supports in any real sense. The simple Italian coffered ceiling must have appeared almost expressionless to the Germans.

This is not the place to describe systematically the formal devices of the late Gothic and the Italian Renaissance and their transformation into the northern style. But let us visualize for a moment how poor in tension and almost languid Italian palace architecture

71. Munich, Courtyard of the old "Münze"

in the manner of the Town Hall of Padua (Fig. 5) would look if we were to transfer it to a German city, say the market place of Rothenburg. We need not consider the specific appearance in terms of lightness and weightiness; the forms are all complete, the proportions tranquil, and the whole terminates with perfect serenity in the encircling frieze and cornice. In the Rothenburg Town Hall, on the contrary, in what conflicts are we involved when looking at merely the junction of wall and roof!

The suspended modillions of an Italian cornice have a calmness in their balance of forces, for whose understanding German art at first lacked all prerequisites. When the ribs decorating the bottom of an oriel—as we still see it in the Freiburg Exchange (Fig. 6)—were later replaced by "Renaissance" moldings, these moldings were pressed together so tightly that a fundamental kinship to Gothic form still breaks through. (See the example of Rothenburg.)

The persistence in the North of windows with beveled jambs and "Gothic" grooves is extremely characteristic. In its favor was its very lively effect of activity—the openings burrow, so to speak, into the wall. The Italian window, in contrast, is cut out even with the wall and is conditioned by an entirely different relation of form to matter.

Thus, Italian columns, in their toil-free existence, at first seem insipid to the Germans. In Germany, columns have to exert themselves more; their function has to be felt. Not that all supports have to be short and, as it were, panting—the Germans also appreciate the ascent of a thin stalk-like support. But precisely that balanced proportion and that repose within tension has never been achieved in Germany. From this stems the difference between the mood of the colonnaded courtyards of Munich and Stuttgart and that of the southern courtyards, a difference that is furthered by the distinction between the Italian semicircular arch and the northern shallow depressed arch. The latter is also known to us in its "Gothic" interpretation from the Freiburg Exchange.

In the final analysis, there is, as was said above, a different conception of matter and of the energy operating within matter. Italian architecture not only offers tranquil form; it also conveys the feeling that this form was *easily* given material existence.

"Ever clear and mirror-pure and even,
  Flows man's life, zephyr-light . . ."

The verse does not wholly fit the Renaissance, but it does denote a concept of the world that is contrary to that of the Germans.

In graphology, a distinction is made between script forms that are easily altered and those that successfully resist even intentional disguise of the handwriting. If we transfer this observation to the history of form, the two principles of relaxed tension and of stressed action will certainly be among the most robustly enduring. Even a Baroque Italian building, where the activity in the forms is intensified, looks still lighter and more relaxed than a German one. The double-towered church of S. Agnese in Rome produces this kind of effect because of the wide spacing of its towers. This wide spacing can be repeated in the North (see the Theatine Church in Munich); but it does not correspond to the native tradition. German Baroque, in the churches of Banz and Vierzehnheiligen, placed the towers close together, as had been the custom in Romanesque and Gothic architecture despite all stylistic differences.

V. GRANDEUR AND SIMPLICITY

LARGENESS of scale is inseparable from Italian art. Everything seems to be gauged according to a different unit of measurement than in the North. The large blocks of the palaces with enormously high stories, the great halls, the wide interiors of the churches—all this gives us immediate assurance of being in the South. The distinctiveness, however, is determined not as much by absolute size as by the simplicity on a large scale. The whole is never multifarious or complicated, but is reduced to a few clearly expressed motifs. The imagination that produced the unfathomable labyrinth of forms of Krafft's gigantic "Sacrament House," or even the Nuremberg Shrine of St. Sebald, is not the Italian imagination. Italian design is characterized by large simple lines and planes, and Italian architecture has a simplicity of form that may often seem almost like bleakness to the northern eye. But the factor responsible for the distinctive effect is this: Italian grandeur is a human grandeur and always implies an exaltation of man in his natural existence. In the column, natural man rises up; and it is he who grows larger in a great hall. Neither the over-tall northern church pier nor the over-large mass of "late Gothic" church structures are able to impart similar impressions. The need to use large dimensions, at least on certain occasions, is not foreign to the North; but northern greatness is really comparable to the Italian only when it is achieved on a natural human basis. This change in attitude took place only slowly and gradually. A building like the Rothenburg Town Hall, with its closely set stories and huge roof, produces an effect of largeness and no longer has anything to do with the Gothic style. But it would be difficult to say how the people who would really correspond to this architecture should look. By contrast, Palladio's town hall in Vicenza, the Basilica, or a Palladian palace courtyard (Fig. 72) immediately suggest the image of a specific human life of grand gesture and bearing.

72. Vicenza, Palazzo Thiene. Courtyard

On his journey in Italy, Goethe instantly recognized this property and allowed himself to be carried away by it into a scathing con-
demnation of Gothic architecture. "Only out of the natural can
grandeur be developed." Palladio possessed it. From the beginning,
however, human proportions were the basis of architecture in Italy.
Even the colossal is not something superhuman that transcends life;
rather, it is only life itself grandly felt.

The Antique art that was known to the Renaissance expressed
similar ideas. The Pantheon, Hadrian's Tomb, the halls of the
thermae, the vaults of Constantine's Basilica—all are large and simple monuments that are experienced only as an exaltation of the
natural. Even when Bramante ventured to pile the Pantheon on top
of the arches of Constantine's Basilica in the most prodigious architectural undertaking of the Renaissance—the rebuilding of St. Peter's
—he did not intend to transgress the boundaries of the human.

73. Halle a.S., Interior of the "Liebfrauenkirche" (begun 1529)

The interior is felt to be "modern" compared to the true Gothic style. But it is interspersed with magnitudes that were not arrived at on the basis of natural and limited form. See text, p. 132, and Fig. 50.

Italy

If we were discussing Italian art as a historical phenomenon and not merely in terms of its formal premises, we would have to give first place in our considerations to the monumental sentiments of the men who commissioned the buildings. Perhaps even more in secular than in ecclesiastical architecture, they provided the impetus for creations incomparable in their grandeur. The Florentine palaces of the Medici, the Pitti, the Strozzi, down the Palazzo Farnese in Rome, have no rivals outside Italy. Also specifically Italian was the purpose of building attributed to one of these patrons, Filippo Strozzi: "To make a name for himself and his family, even beyond Italy's borders." As indispensable as this psychology of the patrons may be for the comprehension of the monuments, we must be content here to analyze the nature of the general concept of form in which the Italian need for greatness found fulfillment. This concept was different from the one that a similar need would have met with in the North.

Large form in Italian architecture is always a form of the grand manner of living. The height of the stories in Italian palaces immediately awakens the image of the grand life of display and pomp. It may be said that the southern climate demanded high rooms. But would such a suggestion explain the monumental portal? Or the monumental staircase? Or especially the linking of two stories with a giant order, as was done later with the intention of further enhancing the impression of the greatness of the man for whom the house was the shell?

The monumental portal assumes that he who traverses it feels exalted in his existence as if it were an emanation from him. This was already the idea of the Antique triumphal arch. The North was unable to adopt the type until quite late. Emperor Maximilian was still satisfied with a triumphal arch on paper; if it had actually been built, it would not have exercised this effect of intensifying the sensation of power.

The monumental staircase supposes a monumental stride and a pleasure in being borne upwards that is more than the mere attainment of the top through a specific exertion. The monumental staircase renders great not only the object to which it ascends, but also

the ascender. The notion of the degree of steepness compatible with
dignity can change (the evolution was in the direction of an always
reduced steepness, just as the proportions of the aristocratic palace
tended more and more toward horizontality); but the fundamental
attitude remained the same and was a specifically Italian one. It is
symptomatic that Goethe, who was so "Roman," wanted an Italian
staircase in his house in Weimar. And the rapid linking of southern
associations to the great public staircases later built in the North was
thoroughly justified.

Man—the dominating glance of a human being—was also at the
root of the great vistas developed by Italian architects in arrangements of houses and gardens. It is said that Michelangelo wanted to
construct a bridge from the Palazzo Farnese to the Farnesina. Even
though the two buildings do not lie in the same axis, a vista would
have resulted that, like power made visible, would have made the
master of the palace appear greater to himself. Similarly, the Orti
Farnesiani on the Palatine are oriented in such a way that they seem
to reach out beyond their actual borders, the garden terraces being
placed along the axis of the Basilica of Constantine, which lies opposite.[1] A country house like Caprarola, also a Farnese building, is
a prime example of the way the domination of the site was included
in the architectonic scheme. The German castle of Aschaffenburg is
well suited for comparison by its sumptuousness and its site. It is true
that the castle looks out over the land; but it does not dominate it
(even though it is from the seventeenth century).

Does the fact that the North remained behind for a while merely
bespeak a less developed concept of space? It will be admitted that it
is a question here not only of differently developed optical possibilities but also of fundamentally different concepts of form. (All northern architecture was strongly influenced when Bernini, in connection
with the French royal palace, showed how a grand style of life could
be directly expressed in a great edifice. He found he was the only one
in Paris to know what regal forms were. We can disregard the fact
that the seat of a royal court was concerned; it was a proclamation, in

---

[1] Why has this never been photographed? It is one of Rome's most beautiful views.
To be sure, the arches of Constantine's Basilica should not be stunted in the lamen-
table photographic perspective so often seen.

V. GRANDEUR AND SIMPLICITY 171

a conspicuously important place, in favor of Italian architectural concepts. The North was ready forthwith to follow it, even though Bernini, personally, was unable to make his ideas prevail at that time.)

The great is simple. Alberti said that the superiority of princes contents itself with few words. It is evident that simplicity was felt to be aristocratic. However, the *whole* of Italian art appears simple in comparison to northern art. The sixteenth century, of course, surpassed the fifteenth in simplification and admitted as decoration, for people and for buildings, only that which held its own in the appearance of the whole. Nevertheless, even the Quattrocento bequeathed us enough examples in which simplification could scarcely have been carried further. To be sure, a structure like the Palazzo Pitti is unique in its monumental effect of simplicity; but such extraordinary accomplishments resulted from the general receptivity to the dignity of simplicity. This receptivity is best demonstrated in the spirit of Italian inscriptions. The short, resonant, significant statement, as devised by the ancients when they wanted to speak monumentally, found an echo in modern Italy, too. Dante's bold tercets alone would have sufficed to keep awake this spirit of simplicity and grandeur.

The wordy hard-to-read northern inscriptions stem from an entirely different rhetorical and visual attitude.

Here, too, we have to refer back to statements in the first chapter concerning the self-sufficient expressiveness of planes, solids, and volumes. The pure contrast of directions becomes a motif. In the "School of Athens," the way the horizontals and verticals are set against one another as great powers has a more telling effect than all the wealth of detail. This is High Renaissance. But even in an early Donatello, the tomb of Pope John XXII in the Baptistery of Florence, we can recognize the Italian from afar by the way he uses the main contrasts of direction—the horizontals between the verticals of the columns. This may appear self-evident with a deceased lying in state; yet nothing similar comes to mind out of the entire range of German art.

It is exactly the same with the style of Italian design. The grand line and simple surface are characteristic of painting and sculpture; and though these, too, are attributes that were not fully developed until the classic period, they were long present in Italy as distinguishing marks in relation to the North. Art is simple and great, not only in architecture and ornament, but also in the representation of reality. It is surely correct to say that nature is simpler in the South. We come upon many heads where the features are grandly joined together in decidedly pronounced contrasts. This produces from the start a different image than does a northern head, with its many convex and concave curves in imperceptible transitions. The decisive element, however, remains the different interpretation, the aiming at a totality in which details are submerged since they have no meaning for the whole. We must beware of seeking the roots of the *maniera grande* of Italian classic art in an intentional disregard of detail. True greatness of style is not achieved by deliberate omission (such a negative procedure can at best produce an empty classicism); rather, it emerges directly from a positive establishment of the value of a new way of seeing. In Italy, however, "seeing big" was the natural accompaniment of a grand attitude toward life.

With that, we arrive at the point where, inevitably, something must be said about the concept of human greatness in Italy as the true support of the grand Italian form.

The Italian Cinquecento created a concept of human grandeur that is altogether nationally conditioned. To this concept, the North at first responded with an essentially different ideal of humanity. In the South, the conception of the great man was identical with the idea of the great plastic motif, the grand gesture. On this foundation, the creative visions of the classic masters attained for humanity entirely new views of man. Titian's "Assunta," the Christ in Raphael's "Transfiguration," Fra Bartolommeo's Madonna Misericordia with outspread arms, the scenes of the Creation in Michelangelo's Sistine Ceiling—these are revelations of a heretofore unknown grandeur of human nature. This new concept of grandeur is not tied to extraordinary events; it permeates the whole of life and even puts its mark on the simple portrait. However, it should not be thought that the grand style of this kind of representation could be transferred to any other country, or that it would be possible to adopt Italian classic architecture without possessing the bearing and gesture that created this architecture. Only Michelangelo's great hovering figures render Italian arch and dome architecture conceivable. Both stem from a *single* root.

The North

The North, too, arrived at a new concept of human greatness around 1500, as is well known. Although more hesitant and more introverted, the gesture of the new generation clearly appears as an advance over the primitives. We need not refer to Grünewald's "Crucifixion," which remains a unique case; the emotions of the Passion acquire greater force throughout. Movements stretch out more forcefully and have greater vigor. In every Coronation of the Virgin, we feel an intensification of the inner and outer event; and a St. John at Patmos, as depicted by Burgkmair, experiences his vision with his head abruptly turned, as if it were a tempest. The expressive faces of the apostles are in general filled with more profound meaning and occasionally rise to imposing grandeur. The youthful saints of the fifteenth century, St. George and St. Sebastian, grow to manhood. Correspondingly, a new attitude was achieved in the secular world toward the weighty, fully developed body, which also became more and more important in the nude.

This intensification of meaning is paralleled by an increase in the size of the figures and of the picture as a whole, an increase similar though not equal to that in Italy. Life-size representation is not rare, and the Isenheim Altarpiece and Dürer's painting of "The Four Apostles" go even further. However, it is striking that the small format not only held its own but was cultivated all the more. Cranach painted not only life-size nudes, but also very small ones. We cannot imagine Titian doing the same. The uniformly large "machines" of the Italian painters require spacious rooms in the museums. With the Germans, size must also always be taken into consideration, in order to guarantee the many small paintings their intimate effect. The situation in sculpture is a similar one.

Of course, we are reminded everywhere of the different dimensions of northern houses. Yet vast church interiors existed side by side with these houses; but this is precisely the difference. The South considered the large as natural; church architecture and secular architecture differ in size, to be sure, but the contrast is felt less strongly as a contrast of kind. The Italians have the tendency and the capacity to "monumentalize" everything; life presses throughout toward largeness as its inevitable expression, while for the Germans, largeness more strongly implies the unusual.

Dürer's panels of "The Four Apostles" were situated in a small room of the Nuremberg Town Hall. Over life-size, they must have appeared colossal there (and the Munich Pinakothek did well to provide similar conditions for them). In the Italian Renaissance, it was taken for granted that an over life-size figure like Fra Bartolommeo's "St. Mark the Evangelist" belonged in surroundings that allowed even these dimensions to appear natural. We do not wish to claim that Italy was unfamiliar with the heightened effect of quantity of the oversized; but even the colossal, which is much more frequent there than in Germany, developed out of the usual as something self-evident.

Another aspect has to be considered. We have called German gesture "more hesitant and more introverted." Movement is more restrained; and expression is contained less in the whole than in individual parts, often only in the glance. But, apart from this, the figure is also only rarely free and self-reliant; rather, it achieves its grandeur through combination with forms that do not organically belong to it.

To cite an example—the figure of Christ in the "Resurrection" from Grünewald's Isenheim Altarpiece signifies something extraordinary, solely through its movement. However, this movement remains plastically undeveloped and does not withstand strict anatomical scrutiny. Thus, its full grandeur is dependent on involvement with objects external to the body—the trailing shroud, and so forth. We shall find nothing similar in Italian painting; even when the body is placed into a context that enhances its effect, it is essentially still independent of its surroundings and remains isolable for the imagination. In Grünewald's painting, on the contrary, a purely bodily conception was not intended; there arises a formal complex that transcends the figure and, in place of the gesture of the figure, we have, as has been appropriately said, the gesture of the picture as a whole.

It is true that Dürer and, even more, the stricter Romanists sought to compose the picture along different lines. However, the old tradition persisted side by side with these endeavors; and the art of

Backofen or Leinberger was certainly more popular than that of Vischer's workshop.

The German approach resulted in an important consequence for architecture; it, too, had to seek its grandeur on a basis other than the direct projection of man into form. German grandeur is a grandeur of over-all movement. The decisive feature is not found in dimensions and proportions adjusted to man and directly accessible to corporeal comprehension; rather, there is a vaguer impression of mass and quantity, in which large forms *might* be included, but which is also achieved through the combined effect of many small parts. For this reason, German and Italian architecture remained dissimilar during the Renaissance.

We have already cited the (late) example of the Rothenburg Town Hall (Fig. 33). The heights of the stories, the windows, and doors do not exceed the customary; but the total mass of the building, with its huge roof cocked over it, nevertheless produces an impression of monumentality. An Italian would have sought this monumentality in the increase of the dimensions having reference to life, in order to convey the idea of the existence of an exalted humanity. In Rothenburg, grandeur can be experienced only indirectly—as an impression of mass and in the strong over-all movement. Just from this point of view, however, the structure is fundamentally still identical to the late Gothic Mauthalle in Nuremberg. The difference in the style of individual forms does not alter the matter.

A similar situation exists with regard to the small architectural objects—the German altars or the German "Sacramentshaus" type as developed most brilliantly by Adam Krafft. This Nuremberg structure in "Gothic" style was created around 1490, when Dürer was a vigorous youth of twenty. Although the older master did not have Dürer's revolutionary influence, he represented an art of the present and not of the past. Krafft's Sacrament House fully belonged among the living mental possessions of Dürer's generation. It would have no longer been repeated *identically* thirty years later; but it can be understood that the psychological foundations of such a work could be affected only little by the importation of single Italian forms. Even the later creations in Renaissance style follow the same pattern: a colossal whole entirely composed of small parts.

In the façade of the Munich Michaelskirche (Fig. 68), the relative smallness of the elements into which the enormous surface is divided is still striking. The whole is large, but it remains the sum of small things—a greatness of quantity. Admittedly, this division into small parts intensifies the impression of largeness of the interior; but an Italian architect would have proceeded differently.

Turning now to another, and final, aspect of this topic: the small is constantly mingled with the large in German art—in architecture as in the pictorial arts. This supposes not only a different accommodation of the eye but also a different emotional participation. Even in monumental works, the Germans do not want to forego the small. Their imagination readily yields itself to the impulse toward the great and colossal; but they are not willing to relinquish the happiness of intimate surroundings that allow the outer world to be forgotten.

Therein lies a distinctive element of the psychology of the German artist. It is extremely characteristic that Dürer executed several drawings of plants with great devotion at the same time that he was steeped in the monumentality of his "Four Apostles." And thus the colossal figures in the Isenheim Altarpiece are accompanied by flowers and plants on the ground. These demand to be felt and understood separately, yet they obviously did not hinder the imposingly unitary formal organization of the whole. The St. Sebald Shrine is not comparable to the Isenheim Altarpiece in unity of conception; but that it is not very "true to the underlying idea" in the Italian sense, and that its wealth of detail constantly induces the spectator to lose himself in single parts, surely did not harm its popularity in Germany.

German furniture with its carvings is to be understood in the same way, as are German drapery folds—to mention still another facet. In the latter, even in grandly conceived draperies, we always find a few nests of small creases into which a more intimate imagination can enter. A characteristic example is furnished precisely by Dürer, who, more than any other German artist, aimed at simplicity and grandeur in drapery.

The most singular example of the German pictorial conception, however, is provided by Altdorfer's "Battle of Alexander" in Munich, with its combination of the infinitely great in its space that stretches far into the distance and the innumerable small, yet fully executed,

74. Albrecht Dürer, Old Man from Antwerp. Drawing, 1521 (Vienna)

figures in the foreground. The limitless expanse surpasses anything to be seen in Italian landscapes; but equally un-Italian is the juxtaposition of a near-view and a distant-view.

To be sure, Altdorfer's painting is an extreme case, and Dürer would no doubt have shunned such possibilities. But do not the Germans lack altogether the prerequisites for a *maniera grande?* Are not the demands regarding visibility, which are among the necessary conditions for the simplification of style, fundamentally different in the North than in the South?

The answer—in a certain sense—is, yes. The creation of a work like the gigantic woodcut of the "Triumphal Arch" of Emperor Maximilian suffices as proof. Indeed, this woodcut can be seen neither as a whole nor in detail, unless the spectator is willing to sacrifice either the distinctness of the individual sections or the continuity of the whole. Yet a style matured during the sixteenth century in Germany, too, that—within certain limits—bears all the marks of the classic simplification of form. Compared to Schongauer's generation, all the work of subsequent masters reveals a new grandeur of vision. The concentration of the parts into a unified whole, the accentuation of the leading contrasts of direction, the subordination of the less essential elements to the more essential—all this produces an effect of grandeur no matter whether it is a question of a figure ensemble in a carved altarpiece or of a single head. There is nothing more magnificent than Dürer's late drawings with their truly liberating grandeur of conception.

However, just when we think of Dürer's heads from this period —the engraved portraits or the world-renowned brush drawing of an old man in Antwerp (Fig. 74)—we immediately realize that the Italian concept of grandeur and simplicity corresponds only little to the German. Grandeur is not absent—the total coherence of the forms could not have been conceived in a more compelling way— but a multitude of small things are included in the representation that an Italian would have omitted. The reason is not that the grand vision is denied the Germans but that they take an interest in reality down to the very smallest details of a single hair or a single little crease on a face, an interest unknown elsewhere. Dürer said, "It is not proper to treat a thing superficially and hastily." Certainly, he was unique in just this minute care; but the contrast to Italian art also asserts itself in Baldung's broader stroke. Indeed, even Holbein's very precise form and fine patterns still betray something of this attitude toward the world.

VI. TYPES AND GENERALITY

1. ALL POST-MEDIEVAL ART is focused on individuality. The richness of the personality is comprehended, and the value of the particular and the unique is acknowledged. For the northerner, this individuality may easily signify an end in itself, so that even with the aim of idealization in rendering sacred figures, he does not aspire beyond it. In Italy, however, the tendency to transform the individual case into a typical one emerges early and, at all events, is very pronounced in sixteenth-century classic art. The unique seems to have acquired the disagreeable flavor of accidentalness; inevitable and comprehensive forms were sought. Whether it was a question of architectural forms or human heads made no difference. In the preface to the third part of his "Lives," Vasari refers to the establishment of conclusive standards for the different orders of columns as a characteristic trait of the good modern epoch. Precisely the same thing was involved when Leonardo, in the physiognomies of the apostles in his "Last Supper," could not rest content with his models (no matter how well chosen), but elevated the rendering into the typical. Thus—in Goethe's words—we are confronted not merely with single individuals but with representatives of classes of humanity. This impression will rarely be felt before a German picture. And as far as the standardization of the column orders is concerned, there was no definitely fixed number of orders in the North but, rather, innumerable possibilities. Every German wants to have his own *"Fatzon,"*[1] as was said by Dürer, who, with perfect clarity, already recognized this attribute of his compatriots' concept of form.[2]

---

[1] Used in the original, *"Fatzon"* is the old form of the modern *"Fasson"* and comes from the French *"façon"* meaning, of course, fashion, form, manner, etc. [*Tr.*]

[2] Dürer, *Unterweisung der Messung:* "But, now, when I undertake to teach how to make a column or two . . . I think of the German spirit. For usually, everybody who wants to build something new also wants to have a new fashion [*Fatzon*] which has never been seen before."

This formation of general types in Italy did not, of course, suddenly appear everywhere and at a specific moment; it was prepared for in advance and it developed in stages. Thus, it is often difficult to decide whether a form should be called already typical or still individual. However, considering the over-all picture, we see clearly that the number of heads with real portrait character decreased in the Cinquecento (as has frequently been noted). Instead, there appear forms in which the artist, going beyond the individual and accidental, places before us purified and uniformly comprehensive types, convinced that the impression of life is not harmed but intensified thereby. We may think of some of Michelangelo's Sibyls, such as the Delphic, or, among our illustrations, of Fra Bartolommeo's "St. Mark." Without being impersonal, the heads in this new manner no longer convey the idea that they were taken directly from reality.

The northerner will occasionally be tempted to censure these heads for a certain quality of emptiness; and, in fact, it is remarkable how, in particular, classicizing sculpture in the images of the Madonna was able to replace the fifteenth-century Madonnas, which were so close to nature and inspired such deep trust. The extent to which social changes played a part need not be considered here. However, there is no doubt that the Germans found it much harder to give up individuality. Northern art fed on the infiniteness of the particular and maintained this attitude even during the sixteenth century, when the problem of typification was no longer unfamiliar in Germany. Dürer had already assimilated the concept of generic types. The head of St. Paul in the painting of "The Four Apostles," with all its stirringly personal appeal, no longer presents a unique physiognomy; rather, as the end result of a long series of observations, it can claim validity as a type. But is even such a typified head matched anywhere in Italy in its impression of an altogether personal life? Of course, a German must always remember that he can read the German physiognomy better than the Italian. Nevertheless, all comparisons confirm the observation that the Germans are inclined to conceive life and form preponderantly from the personal, rather than the generic and general, point of view.

Even Dürer granted but little room to the strict type and to synthetically achieved beauty; right up to the end, the individuality of reality held its ground alongside them, even in sacred figures. When

we think of the others, we at first believe that we have to renounce
the concept altogether with respect to Grünewald; but the richness
and fullness of his characters suggest that here, too, individual traits
were filled out to create types. However, the difference from the
more generalized Italian heads is plainly visible; and the contrast
stands out with all the clarity we could wish for when we ask ourselves whether the row of apostles in Baldung's high altar at Freiburg,
with their sharply individuated heads, would have been possible in
classic Italy. How little of this individuality is contained in Raphael's
apostle narratives in his almost contemporary tapestries! The question is not the way in which the social rank of these men is envisaged,
but rather the strength with which the personal and unique is
expressed.

The notion that individuality had to be obliterated in order to
achieve nobility of appearance could take root in Germany only
during the decline. The great epoch was completely free of this idea,
so free that even God the Father in Baldung's main work (Fig. 14) is
not raised beyond individuality and reality; indeed, He received a
wart on his cheek as affirmation of his individual nature.

It may sound strange to claim that the need for pronounced
individuality is a peculiarly German trait, in view of the generally
held opinion that it was just in Italy that the individual was discovered. Today, certainly, we know that this opinion must be qualified;
nevertheless, it is true that *independent* man appeared earlier in Italy
than in the North. Individualism in this sense, however, is not identical with what we want to state here about the Germans. German
individualism is compatible with a great deal of dependency. That
each person wants to have his own way does not mean that he renounces, or is able to renounce, his neighbor's support. Although it
surely cannot be denied that the Germans of the Reformation had
the more developed sense of personal responsibility, this does not
preclude the existence of bonds of a higher order, bonds unknown
to the Italians.

The grand and free dignity of classic Italian man is in no way
diminished if we dare assert that the German portrait imparts to us
a stronger feeling of an individual and distinctive life. Admittedly,
the Germans will never fully understand the soul of Raphael's Donna
Velata or Sebastiano's Dorothea or of the "Mona Lisa." But the

75. Bandinelli, Adam and Eve, 1551 (Florence, Bargello; formerly in the Cathedral)

thoroughness in the rendering of the individual form of an eye or a lip in a portrait by Dürer is so much greater that a more extensive psychological differentiation must also inevitably result. It is precisely the Italian classic portrait that manifests the tendency to assimilate the single case to a general type (this is openly discussed in theoretical writings); and, for this reason, the Italian people is magnificently displayed in the characters of the great masters. Yet the viewer does not feel equally close to the Italian and the German portrait head, not only with respect to comprehension of form but also to perception of individual psychic life. The interests of the two nations were different, and this difference coincides, of course, with a difference in the national character.

Nothing general exists that does not have to come into being as an individual, alloyed with the particular and accidental. Conversely each individual refers back to some sort of genus. However, different stress can be laid on the relative value of the general and the particular. In Italian art, the single case is always expressed as a modification of a general type—a hand always allows us to clearly perceive the generic form along with the individual form. With the Germans, the general *can* fall short of the particular. Dürer did his utmost to heighten the awareness of the generic and general; but, even for him, the ultimate attraction lay in the individual and unique. The schemata for consistently formed human beings of various types that he presents in his work on proportions was always for him only a skeleton, which was then to be clothed with forms not subject to rules. We know that the northern rendering of the nude supplies more detail than the Italian (as if the unrivaled example of Jan van Eyck and the figures of Adam and Eve in the Ghent Altarpiece had constantly hovered over Germanic art). The point here is the interest in the special form, both in details and in the whole. The finely individualizing naturalism of a Riemenschneider (see his "Adam" in Figs. 30 and 31) was not completely lost, even to a generation with grander concepts of form.

Italian art, however, must not be measured according to German standards. There are many works that appear empty to a German but not to a taste more adapted to the general. Today, the Germans find Bandinelli's figures of Adam and Eve (Fig. 75) almost intolerable; and, certainly, they are also in sharp contrast to the earlier naturalistic Florentine art. However, the figures are not completely without foundations in the past. It is possible to understand that, at one time, they could have fully satisfied a living Italian concept of form; in contrast, it was all over with German art when it found such bodies pleasing.

Italian works that may appear "idealized" to a German are not necessarily so to the Italian himself. At least, classic artists should be defended against the imputation that they wanted to deviate from nature. The concept of a contrast between the ideal and the natural is one that appeared only in the seventeenth century. Classic Italian form was derived from Italian nature and was always understood as nature, even where the Germans believe it to have been attained by abstraction from reality. For that very reason, this art is untransferable; and the attempt to confer universal validity on an altogether nationally conditioned style had a devastating effect.

2.   Leonardo's "Last Supper" is frequently described in the following way: It depicts the moment in which the group of disciples is aroused to sudden excitement by Christ's announcement of the impending betrayal. Surely no one will object to this description in general. But what do we actually find? Hearing the description, we imagine the affair somewhat differently; and the picture falls short of our expectations, inasmuch as the impression of a momentary event does not quite materialize. The figures have something fixed about them, and the geometric organization in itself prevents a purely realistic effect.

To be sure, the expectations of the modern spectator have to be set aside completely—no narrative painting of the Renaissance could fully satisfy them. However, even after this reservation, it remains a peculiarity of Italian narrative painting of the time that the emphasis is on the self-contained plastic motif, and that the flow of action congeals, so to speak, into a *tableau vivant*. This has been discussed above. We touch on the topic again because this attitude, in our opinion, also contains some idealization of reality. It is undeniable that the contemporary German narrative focuses more on the moment, i.e., on the impression of action. German paintings of the Lamentation maintain closer connection with the course of events than the compact groups in Italian Lamentations. And how differently from Raphael would Altdorfer have attacked the story of the divine chastisement of Heliodorus!

This contrast is linked with a contrast in the treatment of the setting that is perhaps even more impressive. Paintings in which the setting is rendered realistically *were* produced even during the Italian Cinquecento; but there was, in addition, the possibility of treating the surrounding space in a completely "ideal" way, without harming the impression of realness and without lifting the scene into a supernatural sphere. This possibility is not open to the Germans. It is conditioned by the above-mentioned concentration of attention on the plastic motif. When Albertinelli used a large framing arch as background in his "Visitation," it was certainly not felt in Florence to be inappropriate to the subject matter—the Florentines saw only the noble pair against a noble foil. It is exactly the same with the central niche and steps that Pontormo placed in his fresco in the vestibule of the Annunziata—the event gains in grandeur but the back of the narrative is broken. The Germans think that Mary's visit to Elizabeth requires an open landscape under all circumstances; they feel that both the house to which Mary hastens and the path by which she has come should be visible. Dürer was no exception in this regard; and the grand style of his last woodcut designs did not prevent him from inserting an absolutely portrait-like landscape setting in the "Adoration of the Magi" and the "Entombment."

Italian painters unhesitatingly also used sacred iconic figures in situations that go beyond the limits of reality. For a living figure to stand on a pedestal does not appear impossible, even to the Germans. The internal contradiction begins only when other, freely moving figures interact with the exalted figure on the pedestal. Should we include Sarto's "Madonna delle arpie" and works like Cima's (nearly contemporary) "Petrus Martyr" in Milan among paintings of this kind? In any event, Caroto's painting of St. Ursula in Verona, which Goethe admired, seems somewhat strange to a German. Surrounded by her band of virgins, the saint alone stands on a stone; and this motif cannot be interpreted in a realistic sense—that she had just stepped onto the pedestal. Fra Bartolommeo used the same device in his spirited painting of the Madonna Misericordia amidst the people (Lucca). The Italian imagination found it entirely natural to keep the grandly gesturing, statuesque figure free from all real ties with the surrounding space.

3.   However, what has all this to do with concepts of *form*? Nothing directly; but it is important for the characterization of the relationship to reality.

German art has a closer relationship to reality, and reality has a different meaning for it. It is as if the Germans considered metaphysical truth to be lodged in the individual, while the Italians are inclined to seek it in the typical and generic. The above-mentioned example from architecture says it all: classic Italian architects lived in the belief that there were only so many orders of columns and that final measurements for these orders could be found. Such an idea can scarcely arise in relation to the infinite diversity of the forms of German supports. This holds true for architecture as well as for the realm of organic forms. But it is remarkable that Dürer, in opposition to the popular taste, took up the (Italian) problem of generic types and carried it through with a seriousness that makes it difficult to deny this mode of thinking citizenship rights in the North as well.

However, it was just Dürer who thought that his compatriots' turn of mind was such that they could not be satisfied with a generally accepted thing but that each one wanted something new and all his own. This not only means that everyone makes up his mind differently, according to his personal taste; it also implies that, objectively, there is greater diversity of valuable things, since greater importance is attached to the specific and individual, since value is assigned according to the strength with which an individual life expresses itself, and since the question of perfection retreats before the appreciation of the characteristic.

The charm of the old German city comes from the fact that each house presents a distinctive personality. Each has something completely special to say to us in the relation of openings to solid wall and of one window to another; in the way the roof is formed and, like a hat, is pulled down over the forehead, as it were, in a particular fashion; and so on. No one would dream of calling all Italian houses alike; we have only to think of the great Renaissance palaces, each of which is clearly differentiated in mood from all the others. But there is still a difference in that they all appear to be more like modifications of a common style. The general type forcefully makes itself felt; and the Italian street lacks altogether the decidedly individualized life of the German row of houses.

Similarly, each tree and each branch is seen by the Germans as a bit of personal life, in an entirely different sense than in Italy. Compared with the infinite diversity and thorough characterization in the German rendering of vegetative forms, Italian design seems meager and almost schematic to them.

The motif of a crumbling wall in whose crevices plants have taken root is also found in Italy; but its effect there is uninteresting in comparison with the German depiction of ruins, in which each stone and each crack has its distinctive character.

Indeed, a mere path extending into depth with a trail of grass in the middle can be presented in a German picture in such a way that it has its individual mood; and, at once, the spectator feels its personal appeal. Even the monumental style of the Isenheim "Crucifixion" does not exclude the striking and singular. No matter what further significance Grünewald may have attached to the form of this cross, we know that it is one of a kind. It is an individual case and remains fixed as such in the memory.

Correspondingly, the entire realm of the human is decidedly richer in personally differentiated life, down to the single gesture. This is further connected with the fact that the unique moment determines the interpretation and, with it, the attendant accidental-ness of appearance. When we look at a Cranach and a Titian side by side (Figs. 62 and 63), which picture has the more momentary effect? As far as the concept is applicable here at all, we need not deliberate long. (To a German, the enclosure of a figure within a contour of a closed and static kind denotes in itself an idealization, an estrangement from life as it is lived. The Italian is of a different opinion.)

And now, finally, to beauty! Is it not taken for granted that that which we call beautiful can be of only *one* kind? Nevertheless, the German beauty was obviously subject to numerous individual modifications. Every painter who had to create a beautiful man or a beautiful woman was permitted to say, "Beauty as *I* think of it." No one suffered more than Dürer through this disparity of taste. Throughout his entire life, he strove with everything in his power after a solution that, by providing an objective basis for beauty, would force all the purely subjective opinions together into a unity. But he did not succeed. Dürer, himself, finally withdrew in resignation: God alone knows the highest, the true beauty; we humans must content ourselves with the refracted light, with an image only approximating truth; and the only element of beauty we are able to grasp is the logical consistency in the formation of the whole and of the parts.

It is highly significant that in aesthetically divided Germany, there lived the artist, Dürer, who asked the question about the one absolute beauty, and not only asked it but pursued it fervently as a question of vital importance. But that he finally had to characterize perfect beauty as unattainable has symbolic meaning.

Unlike the Germans, the southerners believe in the possibility of perfection in this world. Vasari reports that Michelangelo refused to paint portraits unless it were a question of the sublimest beauty. Clearly implied in this is that he acknowledged the existence of this beauty. It may occur rarely, it may be hidden behind partial imperfection; but it is there, visible to human eyes, tangible to human hands. It is even possible to find the "ideal" in reality. Raphael speaks of *"certa idea"* that he made use of vis-à-vis nature; this is as little to be understood in the sense of a supernatural ideality as Titian would have wanted his female nudes to be interpreted as idealizations transcending nature.

VII. THE RELIEF CONCEPTION

THE RELIEF CONCEPTION might also be called the plane-like character of Italian art.   But, by using the first expression, we are perhaps likelier to avoid the danger of conveying the idea of poverty in relation to depth about an art where depth does exist. We do not mean that depth is lacking, but only that it is restrained, thus giving a plane-like impression. Of course, the concept of relief is also ambiguous—there is a relief style that fundamentally negates the plane. However, no one will think that this is meant here.

The decisive traits of the relief character of Italian art derive, in general, less from sculpture than from painting. Even the unpracticed eye will immediately see the deliberate adherence to the principle of the picture plane and will notice it more in the work of the late primitives than in that of the true classic artists. It is extremely striking in the paintings of Ghirlandaio and Carpaccio, while Raphael and Titian handled it in a more inconspicuous manner. However, it lost none of its image-determining power—quite the contrary.

The more-or-less compact rows of figures parallel to the picture plane produce a stable and calm appearance. This sort of reference to the surface can be interpreted as a feeling for the tectonic; on the other hand, such an arrangement will always result in a decided impression of tranquility. The relief conception, however, may well have its deepest roots in visibility, which it guarantees, since the arrangement in the plane is the most easily comprehensible of all possible arrangements.

The principle is applicable not only to a number of figures but also to the single figure. It, too, is placed in the plane in such a way that it can be perceived as a pure plane figure without losing its three-dimensional character. Applied to sculpture in the round, the principle means that the spectator does not have to walk around the figure in order to grasp its content; instead, the figure makes all its essential elements known in the view from one side, in one pronounced main view. (See Fig. 76.)

The art of classical Antiquity possesses this trait to a high degree. It is often impossible to know immediately whether a sculpture is in relief or in the round, inasmuch as all essential forms are assembled in one plane. The reclining river gods from the outside staircase of the middle palace on the Capitoline in Rome may have been an instructive experience for many.

The opposite of this relief interpretation is an image without continuity of the plane. This does exist, although we can of course never speak of a more than relative abolition of the impression of the plane. On the whole, German artists of the fifteenth century were much more concerned with creating an impression of depth than with securing for the picture unity of the plane. And although the principle of the plane penetrated the North during the sixteenth century, it was without the decisiveness it had for Italian art, and the old taste for depth still held its ground. Occasionally, this taste was gratified altogether unrestrainedly, in a heretofore unheard-of delight in contradiction.

We can think of no greater contrast than that between Mantegna's "Death of the Virgin" (Fig. 77) and Schongauer's engraved rendition of the same scene (Fig. 78). In the former, the bier is parallel to the picture plane and the figures are clearly distributed stepwise in space. In Schongauer's picture, the bed is foreshortened and the apostles are entwined with it in such a way that the eye nowhere finds the possibility of building up connections in terms of the picture plane. In Carpaccio's depiction of the sleeping St. Ursula, who is approached in her dream by an angel with the martyr's palm branch (Venice), everything is placed very clearly in the plane. A German, of course, would have chosen to place the bed in such a way that it would recede into depth and would have thereby given the appearance of the picture a different character from the start (Master of St. Severin, Cologne). Even in lively scenes like Carpaccio's "St. George Slaying the Dragon" (Venice), the pure profile views of the dragon and the charger are so strictly adhered to that, to the Germans, the figures look as if they had been hammered flat. Nevertheless, this style of representation was not—from the Italian point of view—a residue of primitive awkwardness. We call to mind the rigid procession-like rows of visiting women in Ghirlandaio's childbed frescoes in Florence. Precisely here, in the work of this Florentine, it becomes evident that this apparent awkwardness goes together with a highly developed conception of space and has to be considered as preparation for the classic style. It is not poverty, but restrained wealth. Here, too, the plane principle determines not only the total configuration but, more or less, even the single figure. It must have been an unequaled satisfaction to see a rich motif like the woman carrying fruit (with the bowl on her head) spread out in the plane as an entirely comprehensible profile figure. We are still in the Quattrocento; but the requirements fulfilled here—as yet only in primitive form—are specific to Italian art.

The classic period accepted this heritage but changed the impression of subjection to the picture plane into one of complete freedom. An internal relationship with the plane still asserts itself, even though the possibility of unconfined movement in three-dimensional space has been achieved. When this law of stratified composition finally began to be broken down, it was a reaction that should, of course, be evaluated differently from the primary looseness in the northern attitude to the plane.

The same thing that we have already noted in respect to the tectonic principle of composition in Italy happened in this connection as well. The primitives occasionally applied compositional laws with an inflexibility that the classic artists sought to modify, without questioning, however, the importance of the requirement in itself.

The strict rows of figures of Ghirlandaio and Carpaccio were not repeated in the Cinquecento; but, even in the loosened composition, the picture plane makes itself felt as the norm. All movement into depth is gauged with reference to it, and every foreshortening becomes truly effective only in contrast to markedly unforeshortened form. In Leonardo's (early) "Madonna of the Rocks," the hand of the angel, outstretched like a signpost, was just as modern as the artful *scorzi* that enrich the picture. The kneeling figure of the penitent St. Jerome, for which the fifteenth century had a purely plane schema, was indeed provided with foreshortening and depth during the classic period; but Titian (Fig. 79), at the height of his development, could dare nevertheless to present the motif—filled with power-

76.
Andrea Briosco

Europa
and the Bull
(Florence)

ful movement—in completely relief-like fashion (Brera). The picture
is thereby clearly stamped as Italian; but we must not overlook that,
at the same time, the landscape is a powerful factor that acts to lead
the eye into the picture.

This fundamental acknowledgment of the plane is not found in
fifteenth-century German art. Schongauer was an artist who strove
very consciously for a clear pictorial impression, and his later designs
tend to be more spread out in the plane than the earlier ones. Yet he
took it for granted that the angel in an Annunciation should come
forward out of depth obliquely. It is not only the angel but also the
movement of form as a whole that has this character; and it resists
relief-like stratification to the same degree that an Italian Annunciation, by its very nature, appears willing to establish itself in the plane.
This refers to the juxtaposition of figures as well as to the single
figure.

But then, during the sixteenth century, the relief style was
applied to northern composition like soothing oil on troubled waters.
This trend did not occur uniformly, nor was it as thorough-going as

77. Mantegna, Death of the Virgin (Madrid)

in Italy; still, it happened in such fashion that the parallelism cannot be overlooked.

Dürer imparted a truly majestic calm to the woodcuts of 1510 with which he concluded the series of the Large Passion and the Life of the Virgin, both begun early in his career. Among these prints, it is precisely the "Death of the Virgin" that illustrates with particular clarity the contrast to Schongauer's engraving. Although the deathbed in Dürer's woodcut is also foreshortened, the total impression is thoroughly dominated by the organization of the design in strata parallel to the picture plane. The picture has lost nothing in

78. Martin Schongauer, Death of the Virgin (Engraving)

spatial depth, but it has acquired greater calm and, above all, greater visibility. The affinity to Italian pictorial arrangement is obvious, and a direct Italian influence on Dürer is indisputable.

Nonetheless, it would be wrong to attempt to explain the phenomenon as the mere imitation of foreign models. There was a native development in the North that ran in the same direction. Even Grünewald's painting of the hermits sitting opposite one another (Isenheim Altarpiece) surpasses all earlier compositions in that the two figures are united in the same plane. And this principle of the plane is not only repeated in the successive strata of the landscape

79. Titian, St. Jerome (Milan)

background; it also conditions the form of the individual figures. The way the outstretched arm of St. Paul lies in the picture plane is new and is not a residue of an earlier manner. The pointing forefinger of St. John in the Isenheim "Crucifixion" is equally new and is analogous only to examples like the pointing hand of the angel in Leonardo's "Madonna of the Rocks"; but, of course, no dependence can be spoken of in this case.

If German pictures nevertheless look different from Italian ones, it is because of constant countercheck by motifs inimical to the picture plane. It is repugnant to the German imagination to yield itself to the plane as completely as does the Italian. Dürer's woodcuts of

80. Martin Schongauer, Annunciation (Engraving)

around 1510 possess, as was said above, the classic relief character.
But every comparison shows—and along with the cited examples,
the long series of the Small Passion are also at our disposal[1]—that
these designs are interspersed with elements that keep the picture
from congealing into a stable plane. Grünewald and Baldung, however, resisted the relief style to a much greater extent. And there
are examples that go still further where the principle is completely
disregarded. Even with the best will in the world, Altdorfer's "Birth

---

[1] Dürer's Annunciation (Fig. 85) from the Small Passion should be compared at
this point to the above-mentioned "Annunciation" by Schongauer (Fig. 80).

of the Virgin" (Fig. 22) cannot be considered a composition in the relief style; everything has been done, in the figures as in the architectural space, to avoid any suggestion of the concept of the picture plane. Next to this work, even the freest Correggio appears bound to the plane.

This approach is always to be expected in the North. The example of Altdorfer is not an isolated one. The traditional depth-seeking imagination was able to maintain itself undiminished alongside the (moderately) classic form; indeed, only then was it developed to its ultimate consequences.

A special case that cannot be passed over completely is the profile portrait. The Italian Quattrocento utilized this schema frequently, without fear of placing the head in a formal presentation detrimental to the impression of life. The profile is a general representational form that should not be interpreted in terms of reality and momentariness. Only later, when a contrast of direction between head and body occurred, did the profile view become a special case chosen from a number of possibilities; but then it quickly disappeared from classic art. (The medallion portrait is not in question here; it is based on different principles.) In Germany, the process was rather the reverse, for the Primitives regarded the profile portrait with distrust; but, subsequently, it was occasionally taken up with great vigor. Graphic art provides the main examples; and here we feel certain that the impact of Dürer's "Great Cardinal" or of Cranach's engraving of Luther (1521) could have emerged only out of the spirit of the sixteenth century. In accordance with its different antecedents, the German profile portrait possesses a singularity, even a monumentality, not found in the Italian.

The next question, however, is whether northern profile design ever had the compelling contour that was natural to Italian linearism, i.e., whether the contour ever became independent as a leading line to the same degree as it did in Italy. We took up this question in the first chapter and concluded that we had to answer in the negative. The question is of general importance for the problem of the silhouette, especially in sculpture. A sculpture oriented toward a relief effect will inevitably have the stressed contour. Germany, which did not know the definite plane presentation and had grown accustomed to a more-or-less fluctuating contour, could not, of course,

81.
Peter Vischer
the Younger
Tomb Plaque
for Anton Kress
(died 1513)

(Nuremberg,
St. Lawrence)

completely give up this aspect of its past, even in the sculpture of
the sixteenth century. The tendency to obtain definite frontal views
and thereby to achieve expressive silhouettes is clearly present, even
where there is increased projection into space; but even with classicist leanings, the Germans could not adopt the Italian relief concept
without reservations (see Fig. 81). And when the tendency is completely manifest, as in the late arrow-shooting Apollo of the Nuremberg Town Hall fountain (1532), the results are surely not incomprehensible; but the impression is given that all bridges with the
past were needlessly burnt.

   The national distinction we wish to point out can be demonstrated most simply in the field of ornament.

82. Rome, Detail from the Screens in the Sistine Chapel

A panel from the screens in the Sistine Chapel (Fig. 82) embodies the essentials of the Italian concept of the plane so clearly that all the subtle distinctions between Quattrocento and Cinquecento decoration can be disregarded as unessential. What is essential for our present discussion is the way the form is spread out in the plane. We are not concerned here with the nature of the garland, nor with the relationship between surface and filling (although all this is very important for the effect); we are concerned only with the fact that the natural *Lebensraum* for this ornament is the plane, in which it can unfold completely, without the need for overlapping or other depth effects.

If we compare this with an engraving of ornament by Schongauer (Fig. 83), we are at once struck, among other distinctions, by the different role played by the surface. Here the surface has been rendered insignificant; and the motion of the tendrils takes place as a continuous inward and outward movement, with strong demands on the dimension of depth. This style was of course modified at the beginning of the sixteenth century; but if we think of a classic example like Dürer's marginal designs for Emperor Maximilian's Prayerbook (1515), we can see that the design is not fixed in the plane to any great degree. And this feature is decisive for the impression, even though the form is rendered clearer by stratification.

83. Martin Schongauer, Ornament (Engraving)

Late Gothic architecture, in its portal and vault forms, furnishes examples of a higher order that demonstrate the same characteristic. But even in the flat carvings on cupboards (Fig. 25), chests, and tables, the overlapping and concealing of tendrils is always aimed at. The new ornament of the stressed plane had to come to terms with the fascination of depth to which the eye was accustomed.

A new receptivity to the beauty of plane composition was, in fact, an element of the psychology of the great generation; and the ground was thus prepared for an Italianizing taste. Nevertheless, considering the picture frames and altarpieces as they are found in the work of Baldung and Grünewald, or in the Talheim (Fig. 13) and Moosburg (Fig. 56) retables, we are reminded, above all, of Schongauer's concept of ornament, and not of Italian decoration.

VIII. CLARITY AND THE SUBJECT IN ART

Visibility and Objectivity

ITALIAN ART, following the principles of Antique art, manifests an especially strong inclination toward visibility. The forms in architecture and the pictorial arts are readily comprehensible to the eye. We have already discussed the way in which the plastic character of the figures leads to clarity of appearance. We have also observed that visibility is furthered from another quarter by grandeur and simplicity. And we have seen that relief-like representation is the pictorial style that causes the viewing eye the least effort.

Thus, the concept of visibility is not new to our exposition. But we must take it up once more as a separate topic, inasmuch as there is in Italian art a beauty of visibility that is unknown in the North, a visibility that is considered not only as a self-evident obligation to the subject but almost as an end in itself. The Italians enjoy visual clarity with a sensuous pleasure, as it were; and the lack of this clarity in northern art is repeatedly condemned as intolerable.

It is part of Italian life to sit and look for hours in the *piazza*. The works of Dante and Ariosto are full of images that present themselves very distinctly to the mind. The Italian imagination is of an equally clear pictorial nature; and the praise of the eye as the most noble organ resounds from Antiquity down through the entire Renaissance. Its most enthusiastic advocate was Leonardo.

Dürer, it is true, echoed this praise; but the northern concept of visibility is, in fact, different from the southern. Just as German art is only partially focused on plasticity and just as simplicity and grandeur remain as strange to the Germans as the pure relief style, so we cannot speak here of clarity as a guiding concept. This does

84. Master H.L., Coronation of the Virgin, 1526 (Breisach, Cathedral)

not mean that the Germans remained at a less developed stage, but is indicative, rather, of a different attitude toward the world. The Germans are also acquainted with clarity, but to them it is only one of the problems in art. Their sensibility also finds nourishment in the unclear, in the fundamentally unsurveyable. In a world of uniform clarity, they feel as if they were unable to breathe.

In Raphael's youthful St. John and Titian's reclining Venus, we have figures that are presented in their entirety in a straightforward view—figures, therefore, whose total structures are made visible. The impression produced by such figures is still within the range of naturalness in Italy; but, for the Germans, it denotes the exception. No Italian would have objected to so much clarity or would have spoken of deliberate display. However, when Dürer proceeds in a similar manner in his "Adam and Eve" engraving of 1504, the rendering immediately acquires a schoolmasterly character for the Germans. A residue of vagueness must be present if the Germans are to be content with a picture and find it natural.

Although Dürer's importance for German art is in part founded precisely on the new acuteness that he gave to the demand for clear design, his contemporaries could still peacefully continue to place unclear elements side by side. Indeed, only then do artists appear to have become truly aware of the contrast and to have yielded themselves with delight to the unclear.

The northern Cinquecento also was a period of heightened visibility, but it could not be directly reconciled with Italy without belying its true character. The magnetic needle of northern clarity points toward a different pole.

To start with the picture as a whole: Raphael's "Miraculous Draught of Fishes" (see Fig 44), like Titian's "Peter Martyr" (Fig. 51), possesses as a composition a visibility that is specifically Italian. The figures, clear in themselves, are arranged in an easily comprehensible order; and the eye enjoys the pleasure of an objective guidance, since the spiritual accents coincide with the optical accents. Although rich and vigorous, the compositional form contents itself with that which seems to be self-evident. The spectator willingly follows the rhythmic line; but nowhere does the formal theme go beyond the objective facts. These are things that, indeed, had never been completely forgotten in the land of Giotto; but only in the classic period did the requirement achieve its ultimate fulfillment.

It is curious that this visibility seems excessive to the German taste. They suspect that something artificial is involved. The Germans do not want everything to be clear but desire that a residue of unclearness be left somewhere. The guidance of the eye, even when sought in principle, may on occasion turn into misguidance; that is part of the truth of the picture. Indeed, even that which cannot be

85. Albrecht Dürer, Annunciation. Woodcut

made clearly visible, which can never be completely explained in visual terms, is admitted into German art.

To be sure, the examples of Raphael and Titian to which we have appealed do not fully characterize the artistic situation in Italy. Correggio alone is sufficient proof that Italy, too, appreciated ·the charm of indistinctness, the rapture that can lie in unembraceable riches. In Italy, however, such phenomena always presuppose the persistence of an awareness of clarity and comprehensibility, of a norm by which all that goes beyond these concepts can be gauged; for the North, on the other hand, it is the very lack of such a norm that is typical. We do not need to refer to extreme examples like the Breisach Altarpiece (Fig. 84) (although they are always of great symptomatic significance). However, the more natural effects of Baldung's Freiburg "Coronation of the Virgin" (Fig. 14), of Grünewald's "Celestial Choir," and even of Dürer's "Adoration of the Trinity," are all sustained by a pictorial concept in which the Italian requirement of visibility is unknown.

The canopy from Backofen's Gemmingen Tomb (Fig. 32), whose wealth of forms can scarcely be mastered by the eye, may be cited as an analogy in the architectonic-decorative field. Such things are not to be found in the Italian Renaissance. They are not, however, products of an exaggerating late style; rather, this mode of feeling, the antithesis of Italian clarity, belongs—beyond all morphology of style—to the physiognomy of German classic art.

It must be admitted that, in Germany too, the sixteenth century brought new demands for clarity in the total composition. The figures are more widely spaced, the unessential is subordinated to the essential, and everywhere, the picture is intended to have a distinct effect when seen at a distance. However, all this is carried out within the framework of a lasting adherence to a (relative) lack of clarity that forbids comparison with Italian art. What we experience as unclearness in the work of Primitives like Wolgemut or Schongauer was mitigated during the subsequent development; but it was not dissipated completely, since it forms a constituent part of the northern concept of form.

We can see this best in the work of Dürer, who felt the need for clarity of pictorial form more than others, and who still deviated so radically from Italian form, at least where he was unconstrained. Let us take the "Annunciation" (Fig. 85) from the Small Passion woodcuts as an example. The incompleteness of the figures does not in itself determine the characteristically northern effect; it is rather the all-pervasive movement of light and form in which the figures are, as it were, embedded. This movement does not run counter to the meaning, and the figures are presented with the utmost clarity; yet it is a discontinuous clarity, which is in complete contradiction to the spirit of Italian plasticity. (In his engraved Passion, Dürer employs accents of light that are obviously contrary to the meaning. These are used in such a way that secondary elements are empha-

86. Raphael, The Young St. John the Baptist (Florence)

sized and the principle elements remain unstressed. In this, Dürer
anticipates certain seventeenth-century practices.) But compared with
Altdorfer, Dürer appears completely imbued with a feeling of responsibility to the subject matter. He never would have permitted
himself the liberties which, to Altdorfer, were taken for granted. We
are thinking of a woodcut of the "Halt on the Flight into Egypt" (Fig.
41), which we cited earlier as an example of atectonic composition.
The woodcut is also suitable for our present discussion, inasmuch as
the principle figures are visible in the general tumult only in frag-
mentary and, so to speak, accidental fashion. These are possibilities
that make the most daring experiments of the Italians look timid.

   It is true that the woodcut always has a more informal appearance than the large painting. But all comparisons lead to the same
results, namely that the German eye does not desire a composition
intended to have easy visibility, and that the perfect agreement of

form and subject matter found in the classic Italian narrative painting is likely to meet with distrust among the Germans. The crystal-
clear display must be somehow clouded and dimmed if the picture is
to be attractive and interesting to them. The Germans are also familiar with the clarified kind of art as the antithesis of the confused
image of reality; but the Italian concept of effortless and comprehensive visibility remains foreign to them.

"Effortless and comprehensive"—this is as valid for the design of
the single figure as for the picture as a whole.

At the beginning of this chapter, we chose a figure by Raphael
and another by Titian to represent the Italian type: the seated youthful St. John (Fig. 86) and a reclining Venus (Fig. 62). Their distinctiveness is not to be sought in the expressiveness of the motif, for
good art is subject everywhere to the same requirements in this regard; but the uniformly clear explanation of bodily facts is characteristically Italian. The Germans do not desire it. While the
Italians are more interested in the body as architecture, the Germans
are more interested in it as gesture. The perfect clarity which is so
natural to the Italians seems a deliberate clarity to the Germans and,
for that reason, always acquires a special emotional coloring. Let us
look at the figure of St. John. Granted that the purely frontal view
lends weight to his sermon—but why must all the joints of the figure
be thoroughly worked out? And the reclining Venus—how is that
maximum clarity in the statement of the measurements and articulations of the body compatible with the impression of living movement? Here the two nations hold divergent opinions.

To be sure, the sixteenth century was a period of objectivity in
the North, too; and it was precisely Dürer who took the lead over all
the others in the new conception of the body. But while this interest
was present in Italy from the beginning of the Renaissance onward
and was nourished from generation to generation with new insights
into the coherency of the organism, in Germany the problem developed only late out of a differently oriented tradition. It would be
remarkable if this tradition should have entirely vanished in the
process. There *are* treatments of the theme that would satisfy even
the Italian requirements, but they are the exception. It is characteristic that Cranach was permitted to suppress so much form even in
his large single figure of Adam (1528). What makes Michelangelo's

"Slaves" look so different from any German work is not merely a difference in quality but a different attitude toward design, an attitude that wishes to leave no possible question unanswered. But, of course, we shall not advance very far with the crude concept of the greater or lesser completeness in the presentation of form. The more essential point is the amount of formal content absorbed into the design, the amount of content that has been won for the spectator, even in the foreshortened view. On occasion, Vasari criticizes the accomplishments of the Quattrocento in this respect with the words *"aspro a vedere,"* harsh of aspect. (Preface to the third part of his "Lives".) In the sixteenth century, artists were capable of designing in such a way that even the most complicated design is readily visible. To enjoy this visibility as such seems to be a prerogative of the Italian eye, just as in the Romance languages the perfect phrase, the well-turned sentence, can arouse direct intellectual and sensuous delight. Dürer, too, distinguished between design that was rich in meaning and that which was poor in meaning. And from Erasmus, we have the report of far-reaching significance that Dürer was not content with an accidental view but sought a comprehensive image. However, we cannot expect an opinion from him on what is easy and what is difficult for the eye to grasp. Still, even from his point of view, he would have been fully entitled to characterize Schongauer's style as troublesome for the eye and his own style as an advance toward greater visibility. The question at hand, however, is precisely one of a different degree of visibility than in Italy.

The parallels in architecture will not be discussed in this case; but it is known that Italian architects of the High Renaissance endeavored to develop form out of functional conditions with greater and greater consistency, and to make everything easily understandable. A certain tendency toward more comprehensible solid and spatial form can also be observed in the German architecture of the time. But the results could only faintly resemble the Italian. This is demonstrated by the single fact that a structure like Krafft's Sakramentshaus, which is definitely not intended to be contemplated in its entirety, was still possible at the end of the fifteenth century. The Shrine of St. Sebald pursues, to be sure, another course. Nevertheless, the connection with the national past is clear, here, too. How little is the abundance of forms clarified in the direction of visibility!

And if the reliefs narrating the story of St. Sebald are overlapped by bars, it means that even classic art was not required to be always clearly visible.

Objectivity in Drawing: Correctness

For Italy, art is a science. It can be born only out of full knowledge, a knowledge that relates to the subject as well as to the nature of the representational procedure as such. From this stems, on one hand, the early tendency to establish theoretically the foundations of art and, on the other, that intensive concern with nature in a scientific sense. This concern found in Leonardo a representative who makes it difficult for us to decide whether he was greater as an artist or as a student of nature.

Dürer adopted this concept of art. To him, too, to represent meant to know. He fought against a lax practice that, without theoretical basis and without real knowledge of the subject, was guided only by an obscure pictorial impulse. He calls this mere *"Brauch"* and opposes it to true art.

Precisely therein, however, lies an essential difference between the two nations. Northern art cannot be pinned down to the concept of "imitation" (even when the term is used in the broadest artistic sense). The Germans aim directly at expression and mood, and drawing is to them something other than the projection of a tangible measurable reality. If one wishes to ascribe an expressionistic bent to German art, no objection can be made. This means that picture and object need not be identical, that the problem of "correctness" does not exist, or at least not to the same extent, and that what would be a defect in drawing in the Italian sense can be considered an asset by the Germans.

All the painting of the Italian Renaissance is based on a theoretically conceived system of perspective. Precise ideas about the act of seeing were held, and on them was founded a mode of representation intended to correspond to reality. Dürer found it necessary to take the same stand. If earlier works displayed more-or-less clumsy representations of space, these were "mistakes" that could be avoided through scientific perspective, in the sense of a geometric plane projection. Some people may have regretted that this science of perspective was not known earlier to the Germans. However, every people and every period has the perspective it wants; and it would be altogether wrong to think that the northerners breathed a sigh of relief when they finally learned how things ought to be done. Italian perspective is *one* possibility (which, incidentally, could also have been developed independently of scientific reflections); there are always other possibilities. We still encounter in sixteenth-century art the impetuous spatial impression achieved by certain fifteenth-century South German artists—Witz' "Annunciation" in Nuremberg comes to mind as an example—where, in a purely rational interpretation, the ceiling beams seem to cave in. What we find in the following century is not identical, but it is similar. When Grünewald drew the small tiles of the floor in the Isenheim "Annunciation" in incorrect perspective, he took this liberty (in his desire for an agitated effect) as a German; and he had the same right that Altdorfer had when he presented the church interior of his "Birth of the Virgin" (Fig. 22) in such a way that the actual architectural system cannot be figured out from the painting. "Correct" drawing would certainly produce a much less vivid effect. It can be supposed that even Dürer did not judge certain liberties in his own early woodcuts (Large Passion) to be absolutely inadmissable.

Spatial perspective, however, is only a special case in a much more comprehensive state of affairs.

Italian drawing relies altogether on objective form; the German draftsman did not hesitate to go beyond it. Much genuine artistic feeling is involved in the mere *"Brauch"* that Dürer censured. A foreshortening may be incorrect in the Italian sense—but if it *speaks,* it is right nonetheless. The representation of a movement need not be developed on the basis of the objective joint and muscle systems of the human body. There is an expressionistic drawing in which line has surrendered its purely objective meaning but has acquired, in return, an independent functional meaning. From the point of view of correctness, both Baldung and Grünewald fall short of Michelangelo (we refer to the classic Michelangelo); but the evocative power of the convulsively clasped hands in a Grünewald or the muscular tension in a group of wrestlers by Baldung could never be compensated for by more objective drawing. The ascending Christ of the Isenheim Altarpiece (Fig. 55) is an impossibility in corporeal terms, but the upward movement is convincing. In Cranach's woodcut depicting St. Christopher stepping to the shore with the Christ Child, it is obvious that the movement can't work that way; Cranach himself certainly would not have disagreed. Nevertheless, the step of this giant produces an unforgettable impression. An Italian, it is true, would not have approved of it; nor would Dürer.

The liberties that Grünewald took in the partial enlargement of limbs are well-known. He did this when he was concerned with strong expression, as in the superhuman finger of the pointing St. John the Baptist in the Isenheim "Crucifixion" (Fig. 39). These, too, are un-Italian procedures; but strangely enough, Raphael in his "Transfiguration" (and later Michelangelo in the "Last Judgment") offers an analogy to the triple change of scale in the figures in the "Crucifixion." But the complete "misdrawing" of the figure of St. John, who supports the Virgin, again demonstrates clearly the impossibility of comparing the two nations.

Of course, this difference in the definition of imitation applies to more than the human figure. Just as Dürer became for the Germans the teacher of a more objective understanding of the body, so he wanted the drapery folds of garments to be objectively determined. A Primitive like Schongauer presents his splashes of folds in a seated Madonna without our being allowed to ask him to account for the cut of the gown and the natural causes of the formation of the folds. But Dürer, who had also been committed to this style as a young man, gradually freed himself from it and forged further and further ahead toward demonstrable plastic facts, no doubt encouraged by Italian examples. However, the traditional procedure did not cease therewith to be followed in German art. It was used and even strengthened by just the most vigorous imaginations. Who would want to judge the grandiose draperies of Veit Stoss (Fig. 87) or Hans Leinberger (Fig. 19) according to objective criteria?

Thus, alongside an objective trend, there was in the landscape painting of the sixteenth century, in the drawing of mountains and trees, a subjective interpretation of heretofore unheard-of impact. We think of Altdorfer and Wolf Huber and of the powerfully dripping foliage masses of their trees, of the rocks that shoot upwards like a fountain! Italy would be capable of supplying little of a comparable nature.

The matters that concern us here play a role not in this one context alone, but in the entire history of art. Goethe had the same phenomenon in mind when, in a celebrated letter to Herder published in the "Italienische Reise," he summed up the difference between Homer and the more recent poets in the following sentence: "They (the ancients) portrayed existence, we usually portray the effect; they depicted the fearful, we depict fearfully; they that which is agreeable, we agreeably; and so forth." There is no doubt that what is said here about ancients and moderns can also be applied to the contrast between North and South. We should merely like to allow the two possibilities to co-exist with equal rights.

Art and Nature

All the visual arts are based on imitation of nature. For Italy, this statement is a self-evident assumption. *"Natura optima artifex,"* says Alberti; and Leonardo calls painting the daughter, or at least the granddaughter, of nature, since all visible things are born from nature and painting derives from them. The artist is akin to God, for what he does is nothing other than to reproduce that which appears in God's creation.

A similar view was expressed at the end of the Renaissance in the "Dialogues" of Francisco de Hollanda: "In my opinion, that painting is the most excellent and, as it were, divine which reproduces to perfection some work of the Eternal . . . to imitate perfectly the form of any one of these things means in my eyes [Michelangelo is assumed to be the speaker] nothing less than to imitate the creative activity of God." The most meritorious work of art, however, is that which reproduces "the most distinguished, the most refined, and the most artful creation," by which is meant, of course, the human form.

Art is a second nature. Even in architecture, which does not depend on the representation of a given subject, the connection is maintained. Beautiful proportions lie hidden in nature; the artist must know only how to find them. They are fundamentally related to the proportions of the human body. It is *our* life that breathes in architecture; and there is no difference in kind between secular and sacred architecture. Natural beauty is of itself divine.

The German Renaissance was also an acknowledgment of nature. Dürer expresses the exact counterpart of the Italian view when he proclaims: "For, verily, art is embedded in nature; he who can extract it has it." But what is it we hear? Do these words not sound like a criticism, like the assertion of a personal conviction that is not generally accepted? Indeed, as devoted to nature as the German is, the transcendence of the natural tangible world runs in his blood. He forms concepts of beauty that no longer correspond to any reality. He yields himself up to an impulse toward the fantastic, an impulse that signifies something entirely different from the isolated fantastic creations produced on Italian soil. Detached from the basis of the natural organic world, this impulse can be intensified in the direction of the bizarre and the monstrous. Even Dürer reproached himself for his tardiness in overcoming the taste for the unusual and in recognizing the value of naturalness and simplicity.

However, what would Dürer be for the Germans if we were to strip him of all that goes beyond the natural? How impoverished the picture of the great German art would become if we were to admit as valid only that which falls into the category of imitation of nature! Dürer struggled heroically to comprehend nature and to bring into prominence her unique worth. But there was, besides this, another art, a natural-supernatural one we might say, which was also current; and it would have been impossible to have remained completely divorced from it. Those extremely vivid ecclesiastical works like the Moosburg Altarpiece—a fabulous sparkling world of forms that presses upward into a fantastic climax—cannot be excluded from the total picture of the German "Renaissance." It is certain that the style of such works was not felt to run counter to nature, but to be elevated above nature.

What is nature? It is something different for every people and every period. Who would venture to delineate precisely what reality, perceived through all the senses, may have meant at any given time? While we nevertheless do not completely evade the question here, we discuss it with the reservation that we be permitted to point out only some extremely general guiding principles. In connection with this

87.
Veit Stoss
St. John
the Evangelist

Wall sculpture
(Berlin)

discussion, a partial repetition of observations previously made will be unavoidable.

When Leonardo, as has just been said, calls pictorial art the daughter or granddaughter of nature, he is guided by the idea of the individual creature: The noblest production of nature is the organic body, and this organic body, particularly the human body, is also the true subject matter of art. The body may be shown at rest or in motion, it may or may not be involved in an event—the spectator's imagination will always occupy itself with the single organism as the basic element. The complete mastery and vitalization of this basic element constitutes the glory of art.

The German imagination differs from the Italian not only because it grants the human figure no such predominance over the innumerable other phenomena of the world, but also because it is, above all, an imagination of the multitude and not of the single figure, of the host of forms and not of the isolated form. The interest in the single form is not absent, but the notion of formal complexes, the interaction of diverse existences, is primary. The "Great Piece of Turf" by the young Dürer says more to the German sensibility than the ever-so-careful studies of single plants that he made in addition to it. The character of the grasses themselves is not unimportant; but the really exciting thing in such a piece of nature is the impression of co-existence or, to put it more Germanically, the feeling of an alive closeness and contact. Thus, for the Germans, the life of the tree is contained not only in the design of the crown, trunk, and roots, but also in the underbrush, the small growths that crowd about the trunk. Such things cannot be isolated. Nature does not bring forth single creatures but unburdens herself in a deluge of forms—an existence in large throngs, which may easily acquire a crowded and jostling character.

Such a viewpoint naturally produced entirely different results in painting and ornament. We can understand how the tight interweaving of forms in, say, the superstructure of an altar—which appears so strange to the taste trained on Italian art—was felt in the North to be altogether natural.

Furthermore, the opinions of the two nations are again completely divergent with respect to the meaningful qualities of the figure. For the Italians, the value lies in the body's architectonic structure, in its formal arrangement and general harmony of proportions. Measurable and inherent in the figure, the latter are preserved even when the body at rest becomes the body in motion. All of nature is filled with these beauties of proportion. Even the architect has only to listen in on the world, so to speak, in order to acquire these merits for his work.

Although the northerners and, in particular, Dürer did not shut their eyes completely to this conception, a deep-rooted bias in favor of movement as the truly essential quality always stood opposed to it. The figure becomes alive through the tension in it, through its function, its expression. It is no longer a question here of specifications that can be taken from the figure as such; the figure acquires its interest and inner life only through that which takes place within it.

Who is not reminded here of the words of Millet: The face of a mother becomes beautiful only through the expression with which she gazes at her child. The statement has an imperishable significance for all of northern art. But it is not necessary to reach so high. We can also say that the essential for the Germans is the glance, not the eye; the grip and not the hand; the movement, not the figure.

Michelangelo's drawing of a nude seen from the back (Fig. 88) which we illustrate here (pertaining to the composition of "Soldiers Bathing") is a prime example of the classic Italian interpretation of the body. Here, along with a complete anatomical inventory, the individual forms sound together in pure harmony and the contour unites as if of itself into a melody. It is evident that even if Cranach had had the same knowledge of the body at his disposal, he would still have aimed at a fundamentally different goal. He saw a muscular back as a great spectacle of activity in which the *"musica"* of precise proportions is overshadowed by the thoroughgoing movement and the self-contained contour loses its meaning.

The important point of emphasis lies elsewhere for the Germans, and this different accentuation of nature leads to a different kind of art. The classic Italian picture, even when it is a lively narrative painting, is a fitting together of proportions, a "collective proportionateness" of a self-contained character like the Italian body. Where action becomes the stressed element, as among the Germans, the impression of naturalness can no longer be achieved within defined form; it can only be attained in more or less undefined form, since all movement refers to something beyond itself. This is valid for every whole, even in architecture.

It is the custom to express the distinction between the Italian and German conceptions of nature in a most general way in terms of the contrast of the plastic and painterly concepts. These concepts

88. Michelangelo, Nude seen from the back. Fragment (Vienna)

are terribly overworked, yet they are difficult to do without. In the present context, "plastic" would signify the belief that reality is fully contained in materially solid and precisely outlined forms. "Painterly" would not mean the absence of these values, but rather the tendency and capacity to comprehend what is indefinitely bounded as well, to pursue the intangible and immaterial along with tangible form, and, going beyond the single form, to experience the interplay of phenomena. Altdorfer's wind-dispersed clouds are not plastic, nor are Cranach's shaggy fir trees. A different selection is made among the things of the world. But passing beyond everything that can be objectively designated, we can say that only to the sensibility inclined toward painterly values does that all-pervasive and all-uniting life disclose itself, the life that constitutes the real core of this mode of interpretation and is as typical of the landscapes of Altdorfer and Wolf Huber as of the sun-dappled cell in Dürer's "St. Jerome."

We place here Wolf Huber's woodcut of St. Christopher (Fig. 91) beside a Primitive Italian woodcut (Fig. 90) as a foil. The pair

89. Lukas Cranach, Nude seen from the back. Fragment (Berlin)

are not evenly matched, but the temporal disparity permits the characteristic qualities of the different pictorial principles to stand out all the more clearly. The form presented by Wolf Huber could never have developed out of the style of the Romanic St. Christopher. Even in the sixteenth century, when drawing became filled with hatchings, when plants and water were treated more naturalistically and the figure lost its rigidly planimetric quality, the eye of the Italian remained focused on plastic values, i.e., on form and contour. The early German woodcut, on the other hand, already contains the interweaving of lines that appears intensified into an incomparable over-all movement in our example, in spite of its developed feeling for the plastic motif. Who would want to determine what is body and what is garment? the way the movement in the water is separated

90. Italian Woodcut, S. Christophorus, ca.1492

from the movement in the figure? where the vegetative life ends and
the atmospheric activity begins? what is movement of lines and what
movement of light?

Light and shade are of great importance for Italian art, too.
When Leonardo occupied himself with them, he surely considered
them elements of beauty; but, fundamentally, he was concerned with
light and shade only with reference to the bodies modeled by them.
In a painterly feeling for light, the movement of light is regarded as
a self-sufficient movement. It is primarily this which gives Dürer's
"St. Jerome" its mood. All things are firmly outlined and, to that extent, are rendered plastically; but this material reality is immersed

91. Wolf Huber, S. Christophorus (Woodcut)

in a play of light and dark which is intangible and through which the interior has acquired its inner life.

The situation with line in drawing is identical. Besides its meaning as an element that establishes boundaries and indicates shadows, line too can have a free movement that carries everything concrete in the picture along in its current.

Who would deny the feeling for the totality of the effect of line and light in Italian art? But that is not the point here. The difference between the two nations is determined by the extent to which the objective world is stressed or devalued within the total picture.

Is it any different in the area of color? Of course, Italian paintings also have coherency of color, but the color remains bound to the object to a greater degree than in German art. In German painting—most of all, of course, in the works of the painterly painters—the colors have much more contact with one another and, overpassing the objects, achieve a self-sufficient effect. The red in Altdorfer's "Birth of the Virgin" constantly clings, it is true, to Joseph's robe; and we can always tell to whom it belongs when we see it repeated. But the over-all impression is still of a free play of color that has no counterpart in Italian art. The difference is most clearly recognizable in the field of stained glass.

The feeling for the material nature of things also belongs to the painterly side. A pronounced plastic taste lays so much stress on geometrically determinable volume that the physical dissimilarities between hard and soft stuffs, between shiny and dull surfaces, are neglected. Roman-Florentine art, in particular, is rich in examples of neutral treatment of material, a treatment that has a chilling effect on the German sensibility. It is true that Correggio and the Venetians can be proposed as contrasting examples. We shall ignore those opinions that do not find even the flesh in Titian's painting sufficiently sensuous. However, if we had to settle the account between the two nations, we still would be unable to find an equivalent to Grünewald's sensitivity to matter. In the range of his feeling for materials alone, he is matchless, even within German art. He seems to have known how every material felt. Wood and bark are as sharply characterized as the down of a youthful cheek and the horn and hide of beasts. The more plasticity is emphasized, the more the feeling for matter recedes into the background; the most decidedly plastic artist among the Germans—Dürer—manifests it the least.

Thus, completely apart from its objective dissimilarity, Italian nature must be different in art, because of the different interpretation, selection, and accentuation of reality. In the final analysis, however, the value of nature in Italy is different. Not only does nature contain the precious store of forms that constitute the material of art; she also envelops in her womb, with greater or lesser concealment, perfect beauty. And to seize this beauty is the noblest task of art. Alberti's characterization of nature as *optima artifex*—mistress of all the arts—does not mean that nature does everything better than the copying hand of man, but rather that nature contains the eternal models of beauty. This is the belief that the entire Renaissance embraced. It found truly moving expression in the words of Leonardo where, speaking of the divine nature of perfect proportions, he says that at the sight of such harmony our soul, which is itself harmonious, becomes suddenly aware of its divine nature.

The Germans share neither this conception of nature nor this view of the task of art. The question of perfect beauty was indeed considered at times. As said above, Dürer's thinking was in complete harmony with the Italians' when he asserted that art is embedded in nature, since he meant the *beautiful* form. However, he put aside the illusion that the human mind could ever grasp absolute perfection. The others did not even ask such questions. That which is characteristic and distinct is more important for the North than beauty.

This attitude stems in essence from a fundamentally different evaluation of the visible world. The latter cannot have the same metaphysical significance for the Germans that it has for Italy, since the Germans cannot conceive of the divine as contained in the finite world. Tacitus wrote that the Teutons worship the invisible. The transcendental art for the Germans appears to be music and not the visual arts.

CONCLUSION

W HAT DOES the foregoing analysis of a very generally framed concept of form have to do with art history? Can we discuss art
without starting out from its emotional and intellectual content?
from the temperament revealed in a portrait? from the conception
of humanity expressed in figure paintings and narratives? Are not
the primary problems those that life sets for art, and can we understand these problems without grasping the position of art within a
certain society? A highly abstract mode of thinking, such as we have
employed in this book, inevitably seems to lead to a formalistic treatment of art.

Admittedly, it is an unavoidable disadvantage that our statements are not free of a schematic character. These observations have
approximately the same relation to a history of art that describes
reality as Dürer's abstract proportion figures have to living figures;
and those puppets would even seem to be entitled to a higher
status. However, it is not only useful but also necessary to attack the
phenomenon of art closer to its foundations, and to attain a clear
understanding of the structure of basic formal concepts. This does
not mean that formal concepts are independent of the total historical
situation; but all purely sociological explanations will remain merely
peripheral as long as they do not penetrate the core, which is a
nation's way of conceiving form and of seeing in accordance with its
general nature. The danger of formalism is not very great, for a
spiritual element is inherent in every form, even the most elementary. Even the manners of eating and sleeping can be expressive of
an aesthetic attitude—whether people mix their foods into a mush or
eat them separated, whether they sleep on soft pillows or on hard
cushions, etc.

It is surely a more gratifying task to acquaint the public with single works of art and single artists; and interest will be aroused more quickly if there is discussion of the convictions that lay behind the tasks of a certain period, and of the society that supported and conditioned a certain art. But all this presupposes a knowledge of the modes of presentation in which art materialized at a certain time and place.

Let us consider Ghirlandaio's world-renowned Tornabuoni frescoes in Florence. We gain immediate insight into the spirit of Florentine aristocratic society when we learn how these stories from the lives of the Virgin and St. John came to be painted. All things considered, these large-scale sacred narratives mainly served to represent the family. The frescoes are a public display, of the female members of the family as well, which implies that each person felt completely sure of himself. What in Nuremberg might be compared with them? Perhaps the Schreyer Tomb, outside the choir of St. Sebald. This is also a family memorial, from the same period, and was likewise an out-of-the-ordinary undertaking. But how remote are these small praying donor figures here—at the end of the fifteenth century—from the proud autonomy of the Italian personalities. What a mood of dependence! We can easily understand that the Italian *palazzo,* with its natural grandeur, could not originate on this soil, nor could the type of the Italian family loggia where, on important occasions, the members of the family assembled, as on a stage, in order to be seen in public.

What we want to say is this: Of course art cannot be separated from social conditions; but inherent in the different pictorial modes of Ghirlandaio's Florentine frescoes and Adam Krafft's Schreyer Tomb are distinctions whose roots reach too deep to be grasped merely through consideration of society or the history of religion. Even if the intention to create monumental forms had been the same, the German artist would have had to seek grandeur on a different basis; the psychological premises were dissimilar.

In this book, we have attempted to discuss—perhaps to nobody's satisfaction—these premises as they underlie the Italian and German Renaissance. It may well be that some gaps still remain; may others feel free to fill them. With respect to the sequence of concepts, we tried every combination until we chose the present one as the most logical. However, we recommend that the order be occasionally

changed. In no case ought one to have the impression that the phenomenon can be traced back to so many separable characteristics;
everything is interconnected and intertwined and should be thought
of as having (to a certain extent) a common basis.

It proves to be very clear that every concept of form has a
spiritual content. The southern conception of form and matter; articulation; the compliance with which matter assimilates form—these
are the convincing expression of a particular view of life and constitute a typical contrast to the more ponderous and constrained northern nature. What a fundamental difference in spiritual attitude is
implied by the fact that the northern Renaissance never possessed
the concepts of the definite plane, the definite volume, nor, conse-
quently, that of the self-contained body—the unquestioned premises
of Italian art! But we may well forego repeating the whole series of
contrasting pairs.

Another question is this: To what extent may a more far-reaching significance be ascribed to the results achieved here? In other
words, to what extent may investigations made at only one point in
history be claimed as valid for the national character?

It is evident that the period of the end of the fifteenth century
and the beginning of the sixteenth was a time of the greatest creativity and produced very specific national values. Nonetheless, the
art-historical situation remains a unique one that cannot repeat itself. Our concepts refer to a style that is called Renaissance as contrasted with preceding and subsequent styles. The complex of
characteristics cannot possibly be valid in its entire range for all
periods, since the essence of history consists in constant change.

Within the change, however, an enduring element can exist.
Alberti speaks of this in his treatise *de statua*. He observes that, while
a boy may be differently proportioned than the youth and the youth
differently than the man, we can nevertheless speak of a persistent
proportion for the single individual. Should not this rule be applicable also to a national body, which has its history and its "ages"? It is
no doubt partly applicable. The difference lies in the fact that the
development of art cannot be viewed exclusively as an internal organic evolution. Such an internal development *does* exist—a development from a restrained primitive style to one of greater freedom;
a development from simple coordination to subordination; from the

plastic approach to the painterly approach, etc. But, besides this, art is bound up with the total life of a people, with its changing content. It is a part of a nation's general cultural history; and although the latter is likewise manifestly subject to certain laws, it generally contains something of the irrational. At all events, the results for art history are phenomena that are conditioned by a number of factors. Thus, the analogy with the natural development of a body is not adequate; and a stronger deviation from the "persistent proportion" will be encountered in art than in the life stages of the human or animal form.

To this should be added the consideration that a national concept of form need not persevere in the same strength through all epochs. There can be periods when, with no interruption of art, specifically national qualities retreat into the background and make room for foreign features. Italy has spoken its own language more consistently than Germany. The former's need to express itself in visual form has been to a higher degree a persistent national one.

If we consider, however, the idea of a concept of form that outlives all styles, we see in fact that the characteristics of the Italian Renaissance—*mutatis mutandis*—are also useful in differentiating the Italian Romanesque style from the German Romanesque style or Italian Baroque from German Baroque. Approximately the same holds true on the German side.

One property of all Baroque art is that the originally independent parts are more or less devaluated and fused into a general flow; however, this process did not go as far in Italy as in the North, where the unified flow of movement was already furnished by the tradition. Italian Baroque architecture also has a tendency toward a certain dulling of the articulation, and yet it will still have a more articulated effect than German architecture.

In its development toward a painterly style, Italy never completely abandoned the plastic appearance of form. Baroque Italy, it is true, did not adhere to the classic unity of form and subject, but found excitement in having form and content diverge instead of coincide. Nevertheless, these are still areas where Romance art usually maintained a clearly perceptible reserve (as opposed to Germanic art).

Michelangelo, the "father of the Baroque," introduced into

Italian art a new relation between matter and function. The ease and relaxation of the Renaissance disappear, and function must make its way more forcefully into harder matter. This is a motif that seems related to the German concept of form—yet the Italian Baroque produced nothing to equal Schlüter's architecture in its impulsive force. The national contrast asserting itself here is one we tried to define earlier with an almost paradoxical-sounding opinion, namely that Michelangelo's "Day," with all its display of vigor, has a more tranquil effect than Dürer's rigid St. Paul.

The same contrasts already existed in the Middle Ages. It is well known that northern Gothic found little response in Italy. But even pre-Gothic buildings are typically dissimilar in the basic conception of the solid mass and the structural members. Italian pre-Gothic structures lack precisely that which constitutes for the Germans the nerve of medieval architecture. How calm are the cathedrals of Modena and Parma, S. Zeno in Verona and the Cathedral of Pisa—quiet over-all silhouette, low gable instead of the northern steep gable, only a faint upward thrust in the walls. In return, there is an already recognizable feeling for more compact proportions of cubes and spaces, for articulation of masses, and for clear contrasts of horizontal and vertical directions.

It is not necessary to belittle the distinctiveness of the individual style, but it is incorrect to believe that something completely new begins in a country with each style. We must always reckon with an enduring constant; this is the national concept of form, which changes only slowly and only little. Because of it, we can identify an Italian work as Italian and a German work as German, no matter to which period it belongs. The customary stylistic distinctions have only a relative importance beside it. The Nuremberg Mauthalle and the Ulm Kornhaus belong to different styles—the one is late Gothic, the other Baroque; yet they have also something in common, since both are German solutions to the same problem. The custom of placing twin church towers close to each other is not the specific characteristic of a single style but conditions the appearance of both Romanesque and Gothic churches in the North; and it also reappears in German Baroque as the expression of a general desire for verticality. There is hardly anything more incomprehensible for the southern sense of form than the pleasure in masses that have been welded together and pushed into one another. But when staircase towers in the powerful German Renaissance architecture are pressed forcibly into the bodies of the buildings, it too is an expression of a formal impulse that was already known in the North during the Middle Ages.

However, separating the specific national characters does not solve the whole problem. History shows that affinities also existed between North and South. It was in the interest of our arguments to highlight the specific and unique qualities that Italy brought forth in its classic art. But who could fail to see that this classic art does not stand for all of Italy, even Renaissance Italy, and that a time came in Italy, too, when the anti-classic elements were brought to their culmination. Nonetheless, we cannot avoid asking the following question: What, then, is typically Italian? This question will be answered not only by means of quantitative statistics, but also, and most of all, through qualitative statistics: where are the great creative accomplishments found that represent something unique? Here we should like to state that, in our opinion, they are still to be found where they were judged to be by those who bestowed the name "classic" on a specific generation.

However, the German problem is more important to us here than the Italian problem. It does not suffice to repeat that both kinds of form occur on both sides. The particular fact remains that it is the time of the German flowering that shows itself to be permeated by aspirations running parallel to those of the classic Italian Renaissance. But that still does not mean that foreign influence penetrated German art like a wedge driven into it. That which looks Italian has its roots essentially in native soil. The Germans learned from the Italians, but they would not have sought out foreign models had a related impulse not existed in their own hearts.

> "Were the eye not like the sun,
> It could never see the sun. . . ."

The Germans were unable to agree to everything. There are always points at which people instinctively hold back. Form and contour became an important theme for German art too, but not the articulated whole. Regulated order and the relief conception, objective clarity and visibility—to these features the German Renaissance immediately responded. However, the feeling for relaxed tension and for simplicity and natural grandeur made only slow headway. Many examples indicate that Italian modes were possible for the North only in refracted form and that they were permanently reconciled with their opposites—the defined with the undefined, the clear with the unclear, etc. It is evident that when the "Italian" values were set against a different background, they inevitably had to acquire a different effect. Regulated order, which can as yet appear natural in Italy, will take on more of a deliberate character in Germany and, under certain circumstances, will appear as an expression of high moral seriousness. On a background of painterly unclearness, the fully crystallized plastic form has to be associated with a mood of selectness and rarity, a mood that it does not have in Italian art. Indeed, we may go even further: It is precisely the contrast, the permanently operating contrast of the "unclassic," which alone makes it possible for the Germans to accept the "classic" as a living style.

Since that time, we have seen still other syntheses of North and South; and new classicisms will also develop in the future. Whenever the German spirit longs for "pure" form, for definite form, for clarity and inevitability, whenever it seeks an absolute value and an absolute beauty in the tangible aspects of nature, a classic trend will rise and the Germans will turn their eyes toward the art of the South. But no imitation can help them. Although they have far-reaching potentialities for classic feeling, but without offering any justification for speaking of degeneration—German classicism will always have to assimilate "the other" if it is to be vital. Perfection must always permit "the other" to show through as a perpetually opposing background.

The situation of the sixteenth century will never repeat itself. A second Dürer is inconceivable. But Dürer's problems are imposed on the German people as if by destiny and will knock at their doors again and again, demanding new solutions in new historical contexts.